Quantum Bliss

The Quantum Mechanics of Happiness, Abundance and Health

Quantum Bliss

The Quantum Mechanics of Happiness, Abundance and Health

George S. Mentz

BOOKS

Winchester, UK
Washington, USA

First published by O-Books, 2016
O-Books is an imprint of John Hunt Publishing Ltd., Laurel House, Station Approach,
Alresford, Hants, SO24 9JH, UK
office1@jhpbooks.net
www.johnhuntpublishing.com

For distributor details and how to order please visit the 'Ordering' section on our website.

Text copyright: George S. Mentz 2015

ISBN: 978 1 78535 203 4
Library of Congress Control Number: 2015946051

A CIP catalogue record for this book is available from the British Library.

Design: Lee Nash

Printed and bound in the USA by Edwards Brothers Malloy

We operate a distinctive and ethical publishing philosophy in all
areas of our business, from our global network of authors to
production and worldwide distribution.

CONTENTS

Preface

This May be the Greatest Self-Help Guide Ever Written
If you have read all of the books on self-help, human potential and spirituality, then this one will bring it all together. This is the magnum opus of all success books. This tiny manuscript is a short compilation of the most important keys to success and covers the major topics of success, abundance and wealth that the greatest philosophers and gurus have discovered.

The booklet covers the secret powers of highly successful people and the missing code to grow rich and how to develop habits for success. You will love this short book if you have enjoyed books by the great success gurus such as Marcus Aurelius, Schopenhauer, Hegel, Swedenborg, Emerson, Napoleon Hill, William Walker Atkinson, Charles Haanel and Neville Goddard, or newcomers such as Wayne Dyer and Eckhart Tolle.

We have taken thousands of pages of information and condensed it into this powerful guide. Rarely have we seen a person fail who has used these timeless and proven techniques.

This book can create that shift and awakening that you have been waiting to achieve for years. Keep this booklet close, study it and become a master of your destiny.

The Great Teachers and YOU

This book is a summary of some of the greatest teachings about peace and prosperity throughout history. Throughout this manual, we will be addressing some of the best success ideas from the greatest thinkers of all time. To begin with, all of these teachers have suggested that *you are what you think*, that prosperity is a result of your overall thinking and, generally speaking, that your well-being is a result of your spiritual-mental condition. The major prosperity thinkers and gurus of metaphysics will say that each of us has the right to make the best of ourselves. It's a natural law. It's a human right that we should all be able to maximize our lives and to exercise our individual talents to our highest abilities.

This book is for those who desire wealth and prosperity. The wisdom herein is for seekers who are open to new perspectives and who want to live to the fullest. This manuscript is designed to help readers make a difference in the world by helping people make the best of themselves and their opportunities. For those of you who want more out of life and who are tired of failure, this collection of timeless success wisdom will show you the path to achievement and the keys to prosperity. Do not sit idly by and reject or deny the abundance of the world – abundance awaits your cooperation and inquiry.

The world is plentiful with resources, and your creativity is one of the many secrets to your future success. You do not need money to plan and to begin working on an idea; you do not need a special talent or to save every penny to be rich. You do not need the perfect business location for your offices. Many people become rich with no talent, no college education, a less than perfect place to work and live, and no start-up capital. The time is now to change your mind about life and to begin anew. When you are ready and willing to improve your life and to open your heart and mind, the gold mine of abundance will be available to you. The whole world of past and present is looking toward you, waiting for you to achieve your dreams; all you need to do is make the mental and spiritual shift in consciousness.

Much of this book is about tapping into the energy of the universe. Many call it spiritual or cosmic energy, or God force or power. There are various words that have been used over the centuries to describe the Source and in obtaining flow and unity with universal power – God, Spirit, the Good, Universal Mind, Deity, Lord, Infinite, Almighty, Creator and Universal Life Force. In this book, I will focus on Abundance, or the everlasting creative forces or powers that are available to anyone who wants to be an architect of good and constructive things in order to better one's own life and the lives of those one cares about in this world.

Chapter 1

The Inner Power of You – Becoming a Superstar

As some point, all of us develop an internal hunger for a higher purpose and to master our destiny during our lives. This instinctive fire in the belly seemingly compels us to think and take action; we must change and adapt. Growth is necessary for the human condition. Finding a reason for being, where we can cultivate our talents and use them to improve life for ourselves and those we love, becomes vitally important. Striving for the personal best in ourselves while serving humanity is an ideal both important and noble. It is part of our desire for a greater good. Becoming the best we can be and doing the things we love to do in service and in leisure is a natural desire. This is true whether one is a righteous member of any religion, or a follower of philosophical practices, virtues and ethics. The state of Abundance is possible when we inherently understand the need to adapt, grow and be prepared. You hold the golden key when you master your destiny by improving yourself in mind, body and spirit.

This codex is a summary of the key philosophies and secrets needed to advance to your highest potential. If you need to learn even more to prepare yourself for this guide, we suggest several other authors: Marcus Aurelius, the gospels of Jesus Christ, Buddha, Pythagoras, Hegel, Kant, Emerson, von Goethe, Meister Eckhart, the poetic Vedas and Eddas, the Book of Psalms, Zoroaster, Lao Tzu, Socrates, Plato, Aristotle, the Upanishads and any great wisdom literature. Then, of course, readers are encouraged to seek more light from the authors in the bibliography.

One of the greatest secrets of mankind is that leaders and

professionals have quietly used the philosophy contained herein for centuries. Keep this book close, use this secret technology and master your destiny.

Whatever your vocation may be (e.g. mechanic, artist, etc.), you will need the right instruction and tools to gain excellence. The importance of natural expression is absolutely necessary for personal accomplishment and prosperity. Your highest form of expression requires an imaginative and resourceful life; it involves the abundance of ideas, things and actions.

True and lasting prosperity has a spiritual foundation and balance. Genuine success is mastering excellence in body, mind and spirit. When there is balance, ideas and energy naturally come from the universe to the person who is exercising this higher order of existence. When we are at our best and act as effective individuals, we actually have more insights flowing to us from the universal source or consciousness of the infinite.

Now let us focus firstly on the great philosophers of science and ethics. These great thinkers all contribute different ingredients to the recipe of a rich and fuller life. Read what each of them has to say, ponder their ideas and then you will be ready to examine the rest of the book.

- Rene Descartes simplifies the essence of philosophy: "I think, therefore I am." With this statement, we must be able to find our being, or what people call their "being-ness." The key is to reconnect your spirit and deeper self with the universe in a way that is harmonious.
- Georg WF Hegel, a German philosopher, also believed that reality was absolute Spirit; we participate in our destinies and create our own realities.
- Meister Eckhart, the fourteenth century Christian Neo-Platonist, personified the spiritual basics in these words: "If the only prayer you say in your life is 'Thank You' that would suffice."

- Socrates said: "Know thyself" and "The unexamined life is not worth living." Be willing to take a hard look at yourself in the mirror, and seek an honest appraisal of your character and behavior and seek greater heights.
- The French existentialist Jean-Paul Sartre was clear about accountability. We should start having responsibility for our actions going forward and refuse to be bogged down with self-victimization and blame.
- Ben Franklin, in his autobiography, used a process called the precept of order, where each day he took time to review his day, set goals and see where he could improve his actions and character.
- Nietzsche said, "That which does not kill us makes us stronger." Thus, we need to face fear and rise above our comfort zones.
- Marcus Aurelius so eloquently said: "Take full account of the excellencies which you possess, and in gratitude remember how you would hanker after them, if you had them not." Aurelius also voiced another great statute that we should follow: "It is not death that a man should fear, but he should fear never beginning to live."
- Humanistic psychologists Carl Rogers and Abraham Maslow believed that people have an innate drive to be all they can be and to self-actualize. This intrinsic metaphysics plays a large role in facilitating the progression of the best in each of us.
- Aristotle formulated a theory of potentiality. "Within each of us is a natural evolution toward fulfilling our potential."
- Immanuel Kant has implied that OUR Perception IS our reality. If you focus your thoughts on the best, then you will attract the best. Feed yourself with things that are good, learning about what is excellent, and these things will build your worldview and character.
- Dr. Carl Jung theorized that one finds their natural talents

deep within the spirit of one's self. When we get in touch with our natural inclinations, it elevates our outward expression. It may not be easy, but if you act toward your higher purpose each day, the cosmic momentum will build to your advantage.

- Both Aristotle and Thomas Aquinas refer to God as the "First Cause" or "Pure Mind." In essence, we come from this pure mind and first cause; we are created from the Source. We have desires and ideas flowing to us from a higher source at all times. What you do with your ideas and imagination is of extreme importance. Your ideas are yours, they are priceless and they are consciously coming to you in every moment. Your creativity is your abundance.

- The poet Johann Wolfgang von Goethe famously stated that: "Boldness is genius."

- Acclaimed self-help author Robert Collier also believed that beginning any task created a nucleus of activity, bringing form from the formless. If you begin something and maintain faith in the process, you may then utilize the act of gratitude and praise, which is like watering a flower with nourishment. In the same way a flower needs water, the universe craves peace, thanks, praise and action, and the universe will respond accordingly with blessings.

- Engels and Marx believed firmly in productivity as the key to progress. The big metaphysical secret lies in becoming one with your desires because you then become in tune with your objective! When we blend purpose and spirituality, our energy then becomes laser focused.

- The philosopher of existentialism, Soren Kierkegaard, was famous for saying: "We must think for ourselves and be suspicious of groupthink, and we should not worry about the ignorance of neighbors and society."

- Remember, Emerson, St. Augustine and Plato believed that evil is not a diabolical force but rather the absence of good.

- Henry David Thoreau believed that we should put our: "Conscience before conformity." Thus, your natural creativity and labor will be fun, and you will learn to freely accept premiums and rewards for your quality services and the products in relation to your craft.

- British political philosopher John Locke believed in a liberal, anti-authoritarian theory of the state. His practical theory of knowledge advocated religious toleration and personal identity. His philosophy suggests that order is necessary to protect the individual, and man is endowed with inalienable rights where these rights are gained through work and effort.

- Alfred Wallace, the founder of the evolution theory with Darwin, systematically came to believe evolution was sometimes guided by a higher power and that evolution could not account for human consciousness.

- The nineteenth century European philosopher Arthur Schopenhauer believed that we are motivated by our will, and it is our will that is our sense of reality. Therefore, willingness is at the core of our growth and advancement. Desire is good and comes from the Spirit. Seeing past the illusion of what seems apparent and acting on healthy desires are the keys to growth and happiness.

Whether you are a student of Locke, Emerson, Ayn Rand, Ben Franklin, Frederick Douglass or Buddha, we all benefit from these eternal truths. The great lesson from many of the world's legendary philosophers is that the individual is an important and unique part of the whole. Each person should master themselves; education, knowledge and inner peace are essential, just as efficient effort is vital for advancement. Growing in faith, knowingness and wisdom are all important factors of our duty to ourselves and to society. Your contributions may seem small, but your spiritual creativity and service may positively affect generations to come. Overall, the ripple effect of one pebble tossed in the lake has a broad impact on the whole of its contents. Thus, our individual betterment benefits all.

The outcome of practicing these principles and suggestions will result in a natural expression of your life's true purpose that will become a reality – you will become who you were meant to be. It will require an honest commitment from you, but it will eventually feel like child's play. You may find many challenges, but the experience of life will be invigorating when you pause in those moments to stop and smell the roses. Life is delicate and sometimes short, and you may be compelled to dedicate energy to definitive ends. All mortals are faced with these timeless questions. What do you want to be remembered for? How do you want to impact the world? What is your potential legacy?

The great masters have many similar teachings about spiritual matters, but the insights sound the same. The masters declare that: "You have within you the power to connect to the universal force." This force is the creative and animating energy that permeates the universe. Like gravity or electricity, the power is not seen, but exists as the all-pervading framework for which every law hinges upon. This all-pervading force is also known as God or "The Life Force." This unlimited power is everywhere as creation is constant. New ideas, new art and music, new planets, new galaxies, new species, and new worlds are continuously manifesting at this very moment in tandem with this Power. The unique part of your mind that can be in tune with this force is referred to, by the great teachers of metaphysics, as the subjective mind or higher consciousness.

Directed thought-energy can be focused where the individual may act as a creative force within the universal framework. This supernatural power is willing to serve you and grant you anything constructive that you earnestly and sincerely desire with focus, action, heartfelt gratitude and emotion.

If faith is the substance of things hoped for, then that very

Substance can also be qualified as the energy of our attention and thoughts. Belief and faith are the same in that they mean we accept what is unseen. Energy is consciousness, and thus "thought awareness" is energy. All things created equally in perfect balance, the energy of faith, attention and mind can tilt the cosmic balance of life, happiness, and success in our favor.

All of us go through life with a steady stream of ideas, thoughts, and desires. Tapping into that greater, infinite self expands our intuitive abilities to best use our priceless inspiration. Thus, becoming aware that we may operate at a higher order of being is where achievement truly begins, and then we become willing to take the actions that provide results. Cooperation with the "force of the universe" and the framework of the metaphysical laws that affect mankind is the path to maximizing our existence, contributions and consciousness.

From Taoism to Christianity, and from Eastern and Western cultures, the mystics believed in a timeless and formless force that governs the cosmos. Most of the founding fathers of the United States were deists who believed in the Source or a supreme God. We are born of this cosmic force, and we have the ability to more effectively cooperate as spiritual and physical beings in conjunction with this force. Listen to your heart and allow yourself to become and evolve into your highest expression; get in tune with the world and allow yourself to manifest your Quantum Bliss...

Chapter 2

The Strategies to Fulfill Your Destiny

Strategy #1: Metaphysics & Spiritual Economics

The fact remains that *wealth* has been historically viewed as a greedy, godless scramble to capture scarcely allocated resources, but that is just simply not true. There exists unlimited riches in this world, and every time supply of anything runs low, whether it be here or somewhere else, someone creates a substitute for the products or services that have become scarce. In other words, thought-leaders and disruptive genius tend to create new products and services that satisfy the needs and demands of humanity. Are we all creators? The truth of the matter is that *you ARE the totality of your thinking, your actions and your inactions,* and that your individualized consciousness affects and controls your creative abilities. Thus, you are, in fact, your consciousness, which is the essence of your character as a person. A great American metaphysician named Wattles once said, "Every thought or form, held in thinking substance, causes the creation of the form, but always, or at least generally, along the lines of growth and action already established." In general, he is saying that if you impress your thoughts, your creative visualizations, and images clearly in your mind, if you cultivate these thoughts and think about them all day long, if you develop a consciousness that what you want is to be accomplished, that form will manifest itself either in you or for you. Another great twentieth century teacher, Neville Goddard, has said, "It is only by a change of consciousness, by actually changing your concept of yourself, that you can build more stately mansions, the manifestations of higher and higher concepts." Most of these authors, whether it be Napoleon Hill in the 1920s, Wallace Wattles in 1910 or Charles Haanel also in 1910, are saying the same thing: that you must have a burning desire to change, a burning desire to do something, and what that means is you must find a PURPOSE where you realize what you TRULY want to do and you'd be willing to do anything you can to achieve it.

Strategy #2: Becoming What You Want to BE

Here we come upon the great concept of presumption, or the concept of having something in your mind or in your consciousness *before* you actually possess it. Presumption is a wonderful thing because if you presume that you're going to have something and you maintain that "state of faith" each and every day, and you continue taking action to achieve that presumption each day, then it becomes your dominant goal, your primary purpose, and you'll begin to create the snowball effect of focusing the momentum of your mind and your energy toward a particular result. In some cases, you're going to have to let go of your old ideas altogether, and some spiritually-minded people would say that you have to let your old self die and let yourself be reborn so that you can become who you want to be. And here's the thing: if you want to be something and you're going to eventually *become* that type of person, you're going to need to start acting like that type of person. Some call this: "Faking it 'til you make it." If you want to be a Wall Street investment banker, then you're going to have to start playing the part of a Wall Street investment banker. You're going to have to know and understand the rules and the laws and the investment regulations related to being an investment banker. You have to become that person. You will associate with people who are in the business. You have to act the part, and that's what separates mere thinking from being. So the real challenge of the day is that you can learn about the metaphysics, you can do the exercises, you can do the affirmations, but at some point you have to act the part and you have to know and feel in your heart and mind that the results you want belong to you. The other critical issue is that we need to understand the essence of what we want. The essence is "Why you want something," and if you achieve it, how are you going to use that achievement? How are you going to take advantage of the achievement? How are you going to enjoy the achievement? How will you help improve your world with these advances?

Strategy #3: Affirmations & Contemplation – Boost Your Vibe

As illustrated in many famous books, an affirmation for success is similar to a petition for health using repeated statements, the present tense and enthusiasm. This basically translates into affirmations or autosuggestions being utilized in a way that invokes feeling and energy at the core of your spirit. This can be called psychological cognitive transformation or PCT. Use prayer, visualization and affirmations so that your consciousness and vibration are lifted up. If you must, hit your knees or gently tap your chest while praying, as these techniques can help infuse your spirit with a higher energy and higher connection with the spiritual source of all. Seeing the results of your visualization or affirmation in your mind's eye is part of the visualization process. Feeling what you see in your mind's eye is yet another step.

With the development of our abilities, we learn to picture our goals and dreams in our minds. We further discover how to affirm and cultivate a feeling that "all is right with OUR world." Begin at home and learn to build relationships with compliments, praise and support. Prayer, visualization and feeling are linked on a spiritual and universal level.

In moments of doubt, practice gratitude and count your blessings. Affirmations and decrees strengthen your vision and conviction. An affirmation or decree can be a prayer or meditation that asserts our prosperous, happy and successful bounty. Many people simply say aloud, "I am whole, abundant, complete, healthy, happy and successful." That is just one example, but you can make up your own positive affirmations. Leave out words like "not" or "no." Instead, affirm by saying: "I am blessed," "I am happy" or "I am rich in love and life." Whether or not it is your reality at this moment, it should not stand in your way – say it and believe it. Feel it as if it were true right now. The attitude of health, wealth, and peace of mind is a priceless asset that even the richest people on earth cherish.

Examples of Affirmations and Decrees

Prosperity

I am the essence of success. The universe is full of creation and expands every day. New opportunities and new ideas flow to me. I open my heart to that power and participate in the divine ideas that come to me every minute of the day. I allow peace and prosperity in my heart, mind and soul. I know that I am blessed, and I am thankful for the gift of creation and life expression.

Health

My body is a temple of creation; every organ in my body is nourished and revitalized each day. In time, my whole physical being is regenerated, cell by cell. My mental ideal of myself is perfect. Because I am an offspring of perfect creation, I am made uniquely wonderful through this authority. My body is a vessel of my spirit and soul, which allows me to exist and create in this world. I respect my body and accept the power and opportunity of life, living and wholeness.

Attitude

My inner spiritual condition allows me to have a high viewpoint of the world. I see the world as a place of kindness, and I become open to receiving the blessings of goodness from others. I see the best in others and myself. I am worthy of success and a wonderful life.

Love

I do all I can to maintain a consciousness of love in my mind. I forgive all those who have passed through my life. I want the best for everyone and aspire to live in harmony, peace, love and abundance. I meditate on the words of compassion, understanding, peace, humility, kindness, generosity and selflessness.

Gratitude

I am grateful to all those who have come before me. I am thankful to the supreme creative power for life, peace, health and the ability to love. Gratitude and a thankful heart keep me connected to power. Gratitude allows me to have faith and the knowledge that I can exist in a higher order of being.

Success

I *am* successful. I *am* worthy of prosperity, abundance, health and happiness. Each day my life becomes better.

Health

A Classic Abundant Health Exercise and Meditation in Eight Steps:

Read this carefully a few times, and you will come to know the conscious power of healing. Find a time when you can have 5–10 minutes safe from interruption, and proceed first to make yourself physically comfortable. Lie at ease in a chair, on a couch or in bed; it is best to lie flat on your back. If you have no other time, do the exercise when you go to bed at night and before rising in the morning.

1. **Relax the Body and Mind:** Let your attention travel over your body from the crown of your head to the soles of your feet, relaxing each muscle as you go. Relax completely. Next, remove physical and other ills from

your mind. Let your attention pass down the spinal cord and out over the nerves to the extremities, and as you do so, think: "My nerves are in perfect order all over my body. They obey my will, and I have great nerve force." Next, bring your attention to the lungs and think: "I am breathing deeply and quietly, and the air goes into every cell of my lungs, which are in perfect condition. My blood is purified and made clean." Next, to the heart, say: "My heart is beating strongly and steadily, and my circulation is perfect, even to the extremities."

2. **Decree to Body Function:** My stomach and intestines perform their work perfectly. My food is digested and assimilated, and my body is rebuilt and nourished. My liver, kidneys and bladder each perform their functions without pain or strain; I am perfectly well. My body is resting, my mind is quiet and my soul is at peace.

3. **Decree to the Mind:** I have no anxiety about financial or other matters. God, who is within me, is also in all things I want, impelling them toward me; all that I want is already given to me. I have no anxiety about my health, for I am perfectly well. I have no worry or fear whatsoever. I rise above all temptation to moral evil. I cast out all greed, selfishness and narrow personal ambition; I do not hold envy, malice or enmity toward any living soul. I will follow no course of action that is not in accord with my highest ideals. I am right and I will do right.

4. **Consecration:** I will obey my soul and be true to that within me that is highest. I will search within for the pure idea of right in all things, and when I find it I will express it in my outward life. I will abandon everything I have outgrown for the best I can think. I will have the highest thoughts concerning all my relationships, and my manner and action shall express these thoughts. I

surrender my body to be ruled by my mind; I yield my mind to the dominion of my soul, and I give my soul to the guidance of God.

5. **Identification and Reconciliation:** There is but one substance and source, and of that I am made and with it I am one. It is my Father; I proceeded forth and came from it. My Father and I are one, and my Father is greater than I, and I do His will. I surrender myself to conscious unity with Pure Spirit; there is but one and that one is everywhere. I am one with the Eternal Consciousness.

6. **Viewpoint Idealization:** Form a mental picture of yourself as you want to be, and at the greatest height your imagination can picture. Dwell upon this for a moment, holding the thought: "This is what I really am; it is a picture of my own perfection and advancing to completion."

7. **Viewpoint Decree:** All is right with the world. It is perfect and advancing to completion. I will contemplate the facts of social, political and industrial life only from this high viewpoint. Behold, it is all very good. I will see all human beings, all my acquaintances, friends, neighbors and the members of my own household in the same way. They are all good. Nothing is wrong with the universe; nothing can be wrong but my own personal attitude, and henceforth I will keep that right. My whole trust is in God.

8. **Self-Realization:** I appropriate to myself the power to become what I want to be, and to do what I want to do. I exercise creative energy; all the power there is, is mine. I will arise and go forth with power and perfect confidence; I will do mighty works in the strength of the Lord, my God. I will trust and not fear, for God is with me.

- Remember that simple pains and discomforts are sometimes signals to take action to better your physical health; however, many pains are the body at work healing and regenerating itself on a cellular and molecular level.

- As a note, you may be able to work this positive Affirmation in your MIND for other people.
- Do this exercise every day for 30 days. Print it out, memorize portions of it and even add some of your own words to it. This exercise works miracles.

This is an updated and expanded version of a Health Affirmation or Treatment taken from The Science of Being Great *by Wattles – Elizabeth Towne Publishing, 1914.*

Strategy #4: Tune-Up the System – Getting Clear

Before you start focusing on your creative abilities and concentrating on changing so much, sometimes you need to step back and take a hard look at your life. Take a look at the last three, five and ten years, and analyze the successes and failures over this period. Begin an inventory of these years to discover the things that have been good for you, and determine which of your actions and thoughts have not been constructive for you over that time. Then, learn to prune the tree for greater growth.

Learn to let go of the old things that haven't been useful and constructive for you, and then allow the things that have been good for you to stay, cultivating these constructive activities. This will clear the slate and allow you to begin anew. Then, ultimately, you'll have more room in your heart and your mind to allow this new spiritual self, this new thinking or this fresh consciousness into your heart.

You may need to talk to a spiritual advisor or a life coach, maybe a therapist or somebody licensed and qualified in these areas. Through them, you can talk through the old issues to help you let go and get some closure and catharsis from any old thoughts that are holding you back. But once you let go of all that junk, trim away all of that mental garbage, you will have created some spiritual space, some empty space in your mental garden to allow new beliefs and habits to flourish.

Here's the thing: the reason you want to process limiting beliefs is you don't want to have a mentality that is a "house divided." If you're dragging along a whole bunch of old baggage full of negative thoughts, such as resentments or anger, maybe some ego-related issues or hurt, there's got to be a way out of this. You've got to make a conscious decision to allow yourself to be helped, to allow your soul to let go of any negative past, because if you don't let go of all of the energy-sapping beliefs, you're going to have these old ideas tugging on your mind and it's going to be your old voice arguing with your new voice. A house divided cannot progress as a new whole.

You want to be able to let go of the negativity of your past so you can start fresh and get that reinvention that we have discussed. And if you have done the work and you've cleared away all the stuff that you don't want anymore in your life, there's going to be less distraction going forward, and you'll be more focused and with enhanced concentration and imagination. This newfound focus and optimism is what will ultimately help you propel yourself rapidly toward new heights and tranquility. Now, ultimately, if you go through this catharsis, then you've changed your view, you've changed your feelings, you've changed your imagination and then guess what – you'll change your behavior and, miraculously, you'll change your outcomes.

Strategy #5: Claiming Mental Ownership & Worthiness

The next step involves really cultivating the feeling of having something already. So, to activate the power of assuming, all that we need to learn is to presuppose new destinies or assume success, but we also need to "mentally experience" that success. Thus, we have to change our essential concepts of ourselves and we have to persist in that desire to change until it is fact. We need to "Be That Ideal." We need to "feel the ideal outcome." We must sustain an attitude that we're open and receptive to the ideal.

When I say ideal, I mean the ideal situation, the ideal result, the optimal outcome. We need to surrender our intention to the new self, to the new essence, mentally, and capture the new ideal in our mind so that it becomes our dominant thought pattern and mental matrix.

We want a richer and fuller life, and ultimately our destiny is a result of our consciousness in the now, our consciousness *in the moment*. Most famous writers in prosperity and metaphysics will say that you have to form a mental image in your mind, on the picture screen in your mind, of what you desire or what you want to be, and then you need to learn to concentrate your attention upon this. Great teachers will say that before going to bed and when you wake up in the morning you must gently think about this new mental picture of yourself, of how you want to be or what you want to achieve or the things you want to have. Think and feel as though you have it already in your heart and your mind. Cultivate that consciousness of having. And, when you nurture that consciousness of having the best, you're thinking from the position of owning it already, as if you were already there, in fact. Then ultimately your dominant emotions and mindset will be fuel for your creation of new forms and creation of new fortunes, and your determined imagination will help fill this vacuum.

For all of us, there comes a point in time when we make a conscious decision that we're not going to put up with the same old negative thinking, the same old scarcity thinking, the same old complaining. Extreme realism is what I would call it, where you're just so realistic that you are determined to be right about what's wrong. There comes a point when all of us wake up one morning and say, "I've got to let go of this." It is holding us back. The moment you make a conscious decision to control your thoughts and direct them toward constructive and productive ideals, then you'll be able to energize what you want to manifest in your life. You'll be able to give attention to the things that support your growth. And, you will be able to concentrate on your ideals and cultivate thanks for all the good and the lessons of the past. Then you can begin to prune the old stuff out of your life and allow your imagination to expand to new levels.

With this new thinking and this new constructive imagination, your dominant self-concept IS NOW *who you are*. This Dominant Mindset is what you will be. And you will have it, you'll use it, you'll feel it and you will be it. Accordingly, your consciousness and your positive feelings regarding your becoming are what will generate your new ongoing reality. To do these things, you will have to sustain a receptiveness **in the now**, which will engender a new flow of creativity. As I said earlier, sometimes people don't even know what their purpose is supposed to be. Sometimes they don't even know what their burning desire is supposed to be. So when you clear away the mental rubbish and you become receptive, you open yourself to this flow of creativity and ideas through your awareness and worthiness. This manifestation of your ideas which are coming from this divine and spiritual flow will be your creation. That is your creative ability and where you find authentic desire and purpose.

To put it another way, your creativity is believing in the ideas that you have as presented in a form that already exists, and your assumptions and receptivity will allow for these preexisting mental forms to manifest themselves. As I have intimated, your spiritual condition affects your perception, and your worldview affects your experience and *raison d'être* or "reason to be," which is your true purpose. Your ongoing conditioning is your power to manifest.

Strategy #6: Acceptance & Gratitude – Mental Prosperity

First of all, acceptance is neither bad nor good; it's a little of both. In a sense, when you accept something, you're not just accepting what is wrong. You may be accepting what is well and good. So acceptance is really more of just surrender to what simply *is*. It's also being detached in a way that you're wearing life as a loose garment, and this detachment, just like Meister Eckhart said hundreds of years ago, allows you to be free and connected to the spirit of the universe or the Forces of GOD. Once you accept *what is* and realize that most distractions are merely material and external, you will see that the only true dominion and control that you must have is over your internal consciousness, thinking, vibration and character. This positive acceptance can allow you to work on what is internal, the esoteric work, the inner growth, the building of yourself from the inside out, and that is the way that you change your thinking and your perception. More importantly, if you can mentally accept the possibilities of good and greatness, then success is always a clear option in your mind and heart.

Let us look at it this way: if you change the way you feel about yourself, if you change your self-regard, you will change the way you see life and how you experience **everything**. This is why a thankful heart or gratitude is so important for all of us. They say that belief and gratitude are probably the only pure antidotes to discouragement. Gratitude is the one power that if you exercise it every day in your life, and you remain thankful in your heart for the ability to walk, talk, see, hear, think, create, it will reorganize your mindset into a state of thankfulness and connectedness to the creative power of the universe. It also breaks up the old preconceptions that are blocking you from that divine spiritual connection to the world and the universe, such as greed, pride, lust, anger, gluttony, envy and sloth. Gratitude and belief also relieve you of the typical burdens like resentment, jealousy, anger and dissatisfaction. If you develop a sense of belief and knowingness based in gratitude, it will shatter negative mental concepts and allow the sunlight of the spirit to continue to shine upon you.

Strategy #7: Creative Visualization & Action

Napoleon Hill, Charles Haanel and Wallace Wattles were probably the biggest selling authors of the twentieth century in success, self-help and empowerment. They all said one thing very strongly. The clearer and more definite that you make the picture of your purpose/objective in your mind, the clearer you make your goal, the more vividly you can see it, the more you know what it looks like and what it feels like to have it and the better your chances are that the ideal or that goal will manifest itself in your life. In the end, you've got to be able to see your desire and purpose vividly, you've got to be able to experience it in your mind, you've got to be grateful on the inside, in your heart, and you've got to cultivate a consciousness of having it, cultivating a faith that it will be yours.

If you look at any Olympic athlete or professional athlete, whether it be basketball, football, track, or any other sport, all of these people are practicing every day, but they're also conditioning themselves mentally every day, seeing themselves doing things every day in an excellent way. Whether it's putting a football across the goal, or putting a basketball through the net for a three-pointer or running a marathon in a certain amount of time, these exceptional achievers strive to condition themselves mentally, and that's why seeing yourself doing something is key to a lot of success and ACTION. If you already have an idea that the wish can be fulfilled, then you already know that the goal can be accomplished. In addition, seeing each major step as accomplished is also a powerful exercise in incremental manifesting techniques.

In the bestseller, *The Science of Getting Rich* by Wattles, it states over a hundred years ago that, "In order to get rich, you do not need a sweet hour of prayer; you need to pray without ceasing, and by prayer I mean holding steadily to your vision with the purpose to cause its creation into solid form and the faith that you are doing so." And remember, the best thing you can do for yourself, for your family, and for society and humanity is to make the best of yourself and to exercise your talents to their highest ability, because in the end that is what will allow you to give the most and help the greatest number of people.

Affirmative & Constructive Action

Taken as a whole, it is impossible for anyone to achieve his or her goals, his or her objectives, and his or her dreams without proficient **action**. How does anyone begin one thing and complete it? Keep in mind, every task has to begin with some act of boldness. As the famous Goethe stated, every idea or plan has to be initiated, and once you take that first step, you have taken an action toward the completion of that goal or attainment of that dream. So each day we have to do all we can to achieve that particular goal. We have to do all we can in the present moment and stay focused one step at a time toward the incremental achievement of a particular objective. And I think that's what people mean by the concept of "24 hours a day." You don't have yesterday, you don't have tomorrow; what you have is today. All we have is right now and it's a gift, and if you can focus your mind and your attention on the actions that you need to do now and get them done effectively and efficiently, then you are destined to become great and destined to have a richer and fuller life.

If you don't know how to begin, take out a pen and paper and write down three things that you can do tomorrow, the three most important things that you can do tomorrow toward the attainment of your dream. And if you can't do all three tomorrow, it doesn't matter. But remember, each day you can do three things for the betterment of yourself, the betterment of your family and the betterment of society. And at the end of the day, if you do three things a day, you will have done over 1,000 actions in one year toward making yourself a better person, developing self-regard and building yourself up from the inside out. At the end of one year, believe me, people will see the difference. Further, with writing things down, this habit imprints aspirations on the subconscious to work on and sort out while awake and sleeping. Thus, the process of writing down lists of tasks embeds the action plan in the mind so that ideas become a purpose-backed objective to work on, or at least to cultivate.

Being Excellent in Your Daily Activities

Many great writers talk about value and increase or giving without expectation, and all of these things are key virtues in the expansion and improvement of your life. What these authors mean by value and **increase** is that if you provide excellence to other people, then you will be known as excellent and as a person who increases the lives of others. If you give someone quality service with that extra little something, go the extra mile, you will be remembered well by all people. All these acts of excellence and increase in value, one by one, convey the impression to other people that you have the ability to provide advice, services and products with skill, diligence and enthusiasm. All of this adds up, and you will become rich in life, you will become great and you will become a shining star as a result of these metaphysical practices.

Chapter 3

The Power of the Present – Presumption Decoded

Being Contemplative in Action – Getting Into NOW

If you have ever thought deeply about the magical power of the present moment, you may wonder if you have the capability for this type of superior focus and mindfulness. After reviewing all of the major religions on the philosophy of the power of PRESENCE, I have discovered many specific keys to success to being in the moment. To begin with, the theme of the Power of Awareness is to quiet the mind, calm the self-talk and learn to control your thoughts while directing your thinking so that you may be present in the moment, to be alive and conscious "right now."

This is not necessarily an Eastern or Western concept; however, there are many esoteric and Christian underpinnings herein that are addressed. Firstly, it is advised that we intently listen to our self-talk deep within our mind and then try to truly see and listen to that inner voice as an observer. Getting to know your ego voice as compared to the authentic spiritual voice of your heart is also a major exercise of this topic.

The easiest example of directing your awareness to the now is to direct your controlled attentiveness to your body, to your breathing, to what you see, what you hear, what you're eating or what you're tasting or who you're with. Whether it's focusing on your child's vitality or actually seeing or sensing parts of your own body, you can go deeper into your awareness. Here's an example. Try to actually feel your extremities, actually noticing the feelings in your fingers or feelings in your toes at any given moment. Also try discovering what emotions are going on in your mind or even in your stomach.

If you're like the average person, your mind could be harping on 50 different things at once, like a TV showing 50 different channels constantly running, and the real key is to pick a channel and focus on it, on a single concept, one thing at a time, one moment at a time, one day at a time, one instance at a time. Further, we can concentrate on one thing at a time or we can just be aware of the moment and allow our mind to do what is best for us. As an example, in the famous movie *The Last Samurai* with Tom Cruise, it talks about no mind. To NOT overthink everything is what a teacher would mean by no mind, not overanalyzing every single move or every single tactic. And just like driving, the first time you drive the car or use a stick shift, there are many things that you're learning how to do that sooner or later become embedded in your subconscious or in your muscle memory, turning them into automatic actions, such as when you get into a car and know exactly what you need to do without consciously thinking about it. So the key really is to be able to program the way you live to think and live in a way that doesn't require you to overanalyze everything. This process allows you to exist in your real-time state of aliveness.

After rereading books on mysticism and self-empowerment, many of us have an awakening of consciousness, a spiritual awakening of sorts, and don't even know how it happened or what had happened, and years later we figure out that as a byproduct of reading what other mystics had taught about these types of transformations, we became better people.

However, there are many of us out here in the world who have already had this similar type of awakening, this aliveness, this consciousness, and if you are one of us, you know it deeply. If you're on an enlightened path, you will inherently know it because you can walk into a room with 100 people in it, and you can look around and actually see people, feeling like you're actually alive and you know what is happening around you. If you're living in this realm of awareness, you will have the ability to control what's going on in your mind and your thoughts, and you will have the ability to choose and decide the type of thinking that you will have all day long. In the end, the type of thinking that you have all day long, the type of actions you do all day long, IS the person who you ARE, or who you are becoming. Then that's who and what you REALLY are. That is what you will become.

In total, if you're able to control your thinking and you're able to control who you are and the totality of your actions and inactions, then you're entirely able to control your destiny and you're able to control what you become.

In books such as *Meditations* by Marcus Aurelius, *On Detachment* by Meister Eckhart, or *The Power of Now* by Eckhart Tolle, the authors discuss key issues such as "detachment," "no mind" and "pain body." I'm going to explain these concepts to you right now. Detachment may be a simple way of saying the following: If you are a person who is sitting around each day thinking negative and destructive thoughts, trying to be the victim and trying to identify with all the unfairness around you, your mind is clouded with pain. If you complain all of the time while also trying to blame everyone except yourself for the situation, then that is the pain body. You can learn about ego-related psychological issues in church, in therapy, in temples, from a life coach, or in various spiritual venues.

What I'm saying is that if you have this ego that's wrapped up in its own identity and it's trying to protect itself, it's not going to want to take a look in the mirror. Your ego is not going to want to change. It's not going to want to accept responsibility for your life and the way you are and what's become of you. Breaking free of that bondage allows you to find your spiritual self, your true inner self, who you really are and lets you get in touch with that and get in touch with the spirituality within. Then, all of a sudden, this unlimited flow and this unlimited potentiality become available to you, and that's where this aliveness comes from. That's what the Christians talk about as being *contemplative in action*. Christians also talk about the Holy Spirit, which is basically that connectedness and that non-separateness, that *spiritual, god-unity* that every faith around the world speaks of in relation to illumination.

Once you enter this aliveness and this newfound awakening in consciousness, you'll have no need to constantly defend yourself mentally or overtly. You'll have no desire to overreact to things. You'll have this true power within. A new consciousness will bloom inside you, which determines how you effectively manifest life's journey. By and large, if you're able to develop a new consciousness of aliveness, a higher consciousness of success, a greater consciousness of action and doing things, this *"in the moment"* consciousness is what will transmute ideas into success and transform possibility into mental form, bringing ideas into material, tangible form on this earthly plane.

In many other religions or spiritual movements, you'll hear the word "acceptance" and being able to accept what is. Groups may espouse, "Accept the now or accept the good or accept the bad and let go of it." Generally, this is what will free you from the present attitude that is saying that you should struggle or be a victim. Furthermore, this bold idea of knowingness is what you really want. You want to know and believe that you could control your destiny, and if you don't know and you don't believe, then you might be sitting around wishing for something to happen or hoping for something to happen, and it can keep you stuck in the past or stuck wishing in the future.

False hope can keep you from realizing your dreams if your ego and your "self" is so identified with what is wrong with YOUR world. If you can change your train of thought and change how you think, you'll be able to allow your mind to focus on what is right with the world and look at what is good and what is beautiful. If you start focusing on all the good and the beauty or the *rightness* and the righteousness of the world along with the universe's impersonal laws and bountiful nature, you'll be able to see and attract more of what is good, right, and wholesome into your stream of thought.

In essence, your personal development and self-regard is an inside job. Transformation to a higher order is a quantum-spiritual science. This mystical power is also the power of consciousness and being connected, and being able to control what goes on inside your consciousness is esoteric. This science is what spiritual, religious and philosophical leaders have been talking about since Pythagoras, Socrates, Plato, Confucius, Buddha, Aristotle and all the rest. The great teachers have been talking about these metaphysical-scientific concepts since the beginning of civilization. If you can master yourself, you'll be able to master your destiny and have a great effect upon those around you while also doing a great service for humanity.

The sheer benefits of "The Power of Consciousness" or being aware "in the present moment" are these facts. This power allows you to compartmentalize the day, which keeps you from being paralyzed by any non-urgent situations, and you're able to free the mind of attachments. If you can free the mind of too much junk that's floating around in it, you'll be able to focus and concentrate and direct your energies into the areas that will most improve your life from the inside out.

Additionally, attention is energy, so you need to remember that what you focus on is what expands in your life. Choose and decide what to energize with your attention in any given moment. As I said before, the pain body is this negative energy of the ego mind, and if you're able to get your attention away from that and give your attention to things that are constructive and positive and reinvigorating, then that's what you want to do. Give your attention to the pain body and guess what will happen? That fuel will keep pain flowing and going. Those who teach about the power of the PRESENT also write a lot about how your conscious mind and your subconscious mind coexist, or rather, how to transcend your ego self to begin to listen to your spiritual voice.

It's like this: all of us really need to tap into our spiritual self, which is basically the best friend that you always imagined as a child. Now you know that there's an old adage that says that some children have their little best friend, their *imaginary* friend, which is really their spiritual-higher self that they are embracing and befriending, and their imagination allows them to love that part of their "spiritual self" without limitation. This connection allows many to be connected to their authentic voice. However, a lot of children lose this magical relationship at a very early age.

We know this story. We've seen it time and time again, so we know that this spiritual self, this best friend, that's the authentic relationship that we need to cultivate. The relationship with our spiritual self and our relationship with the *spirit of the universe* should come first for us so that we may maximize our peace and prosperity.

Some of these famous authors of "days gone by" have said that when you have a grateful mind and a thankful heart it is a lot easier to maintain a living faith. Thus, a mind of joy cannot support a "blame/victim mindset" or negative thinking. So the best thing that we can all do for ourselves to change our worldview is to revolutionize how we think and change our state of gratefulness. As the famous philosopher Magus Incognito once said, each person's worldview is based on his or her spiritual condition, and this worldview hinges on the gratitude and faith that we cultivate.

The word "alchemy" really means transmuting one substance into another substance, and if you could transform your lower self into your higher self thinking, if you could transcend from your ego toward your spiritual essence, that is the real key to these teachings. Transmutation is achieved by the conscious unity with the spirit of the universe. Transmutation is achieved through the consciousness of love, the consciousness of wisdom, the consciousness of gratitude and joy.

The next issue in the power of the moment is how many of us are addicted to the adrenaline of anger, self-righteousness, justified anger and blame. Unfortunately, that's why social justice has become such a trendy thing – because it can get you so riled up blaming somebody for something that happened a long time ago, when in essence, if we focused all that very same time and energy on inner social justice, our views of society would transform. Thus, the whole world consciousness would probably change for the better.

Obsession with negativity is a danger we face if we surround ourselves with angry people, people who are not alive with faith, people who are pessimistic-realists, or who think the whole world is bad. This type of attitude is contagious, and regrettably, as spiritual seekers, we want to be close to those who want a spiritual life. If we can draw close to those who have the same general desire of wholeness and aliveness and health, then we will all become healthier much quicker, and this of course is why self-help groups and fellowships of all sorts have become so popular over the last 30, 40, 50 years. This earnest desire for healing, faith, wholeness and happiness constitutes a curative vibration that has been proven to put various diseases into remission.

The theme of "Real Time Consciousness" is correlated to being in flow and allowing detachment. The great Rhineland Mystic, Meister Eckhart, talked a lot about detachment. We're talking about nonresistance and being in tune with Spirit, and there's just so many times in our lives when we can just let go, stay connected and thrive. Accordingly, some of the biggest miracles in our lives happen when we're not fighting something, we have our mouths shut and we just allow things to unfold. We have to know when to FLOW and when to pick our battles and know when to stand up for ourselves, but, in general, 99 percent of the time we're going to be okay if we can just stay calm, do our best in the moment, and allow people just to be.

Once you have developed this aliveness, this consciousness and this higher order in your life, you will know what it feels like and you're going to want more of this genuine exhilaration. You're going to do the things that you must do to stay in tune and embrace and own this newfound power, because it feels so good to be alive and to be clear. Further, if we keep our minds somewhat clear and we do the things we need to do each day or each week to maintain that spirit, that clarity and that peace of mind will be available and afforded to us.

In the end, this chapter is about surrender. It's about "surrendering to win." If you let go of the things that are hurting you, you will be able to move forward where you do not need to drag around a lot of dead weight along with you anymore. You will be more free, more clear and more nimble. Only then will you learn to act with purpose and clarity and focus because you're not carrying all this excess baggage. You will learn to do all you can in the now, and this surrender really unveils your spiritual power.

So, in essence, a lot of religions, movements, and spiritual groups talk about this key to the power of freeing and clearing the mind. When you're able to master yourself, you're able to let go of all the junk from the past, you're able to create this space inside of you and allow joy, faith, wholeness and greatness to come into your heart for the first time.

Some people refer to this process as creating a spiritual vacuum, and this vacuum, once you have cleared away the old mental baggage, creates space where something has to fill it. This is where the miracle begins and you can fill the space with love, aliveness, joy, and enthusiasm. Being in the "power of the moment" lets you have this consciousness of good where you believe and you know that the world will take care of you in spite of everything that's going on, and then good things will come to you. Good people, good ideas, good opportunities, good health and so forth will all be available to you.

So, in summary, this new Consciousness involves developing a relaxed and free awareness of the now, IN the moment. In this higher awareness, you may now become receptive and awake to the good and the beautiful things in the world such as gratitude, health, aliveness, optimism, knowingness and your "I am-ness" where your "spiritual and divine energy/presence" is made available to you. What is the "I am"? The "I am" is your presence where you know you are connected to power. It is your *unified spirit* that is talked about in the old wisdom literature.

For many seekers, this is the moment of transformation: when you wake up one morning, after having been engaged in gratitude in your daily life, and you are free from the mental baggage of your past and you are consciously using these methods and these steps of developing clarity, and behold, one morning YOU WAKE UP, and you're MENTALLY on the RIGHT side of the bed. A few days later, if you keep practicing this consciousness of love and consciousness of God and consciousness of gratitude, you wake up again like that. Then, all of a sudden you'll continue to wake up on the right side of the bed for a few consecutive days, and you now look forward to the day. You'll be alive and will want to do things each day for yourself and other people and participate in life. And thus, you go from hope to faith, and from faith to KNOWING. And all of this aliveness and that now-ness and that spiritual awakeness is what dissipates this pain body and this negative thinking.

In conclusion, once you become awake, you're going to be so thrilled and energized by it that you're going to feel reinvented. You're going to want to repudiate generalized negative thinking, and if you hear other people being negative and pessimistic and wasteful, then you're not going to want to be around them.

If you hear your own voice in your mind and you're observing your mind complaining and trying to justify and blame, you will be inclined to tell it to stop. You're going to want to wake up to be alive, in tune with the infinite and connected to the world, and you're going to want to be aware to see the beauty of life, regardless of what bad things happen.

Unfortunately, we all have had some big challenges in life. I've gone through tragedies like Hurricane Katrina. I've lost loved ones, including close family members. I've lost businesses, had greedy people steal from me, and I've had burdens just like everyone else. I've had losses and defeats and pain and real catastrophic events in my life, but when you achieve this aliveness and this consciousness of now, you know that you can move on and you can prevail to go to greater heights regardless of what happens. This is because you truly have yourself and you have your unity, your empowerment and your earnest connection to the Spirit of the Universe.

Chapter 4

The Twelve-Fold Path of Prosperity™

In this age of a fast-paced and high-tech world, people are, more and more, seeking a strategic path to authentic health, inner peace, better careers and success. Becoming a warrior at true peace with yourself is the first key to happiness. Bridging your actions to your spiritual mind and body is where success can naturally emerge. To manifest a greater destiny, a person must make an informed inventory of their assets and desires. Each of us must: 1) Analyze the results of our recent track record; 2) Make a diagnosis of what tactics are good or bad; 3) Create a plan to improve our lives on mental, physical and spiritual levels; 4) Implement the new strategic actions; 5) Monitor the ongoing results; and 6) Take corrective measures from time to time. To implement a new plan, we must form a clear and definite mental image of the results that we wish to have to achieve or see the ideal image of what we want to become. The seeker must cultivate his or her new beliefs using a higher order of imagination so as to feel worthy of greater heights. Throughout these 12 steps below, we will discuss the keys to joy, flow, excellence, peace and abundance. The person who wants to have an abundant life and prosperity must accurately develop his or her purpose and learn to imagine living the life that he or she would want to live. A true seeker of prosperity will learn to see their presumed destinies with an earnest thanksgiving that his new reality is manifesting.

This is the methodology by which mental energy or mental impressions are transferred over to the universe, and the creative forces are set in motion like a tiny chain reaction of activity. Each of us must use proper attention and concentration intertwined with a harmonious mind, faith and gratitude that is all rooted in love. Your higher consciousness will then begin working with you to allow greater attention, concentration and natural expression on a higher level. Defining your purpose in life or aiming toward specific outcomes while letting them unfold in the best ways will be where the miracles appear. Moreover, allowing your talents, true place and right career to expand will also be a powerful part of your journey. Ultimately, developing stronger concentration, thoughts, speech and a greater worldview to support your actions and goals will be the catalyst of newfound successes. Combining the awakened mind with action is where your results begin to appear and build momentum toward tremendous growth and expansion.

1. Constructive Motives with Attentiveness

The first principles of the path, attention and concentration, are described as a laser focusing of the mind, which is a state in which all cognitive faculties are unified and directed to a particular objective. This is not simply being aware of your environment, but being conscious of your thought energy. By thinking, an earnest desire is brought to you, and by acting, you bring the desire into reality. While staying focused with faith and purpose, imagine your desired objective with all your heart and with all your strength and with all your concentration. Hold the vision of yourself with the highest and best result on the picture screen of your mind. Next, use your current abilities or position as a means of developing yourself and continuous improvement. Keeping a vision of your purpose or goal held with confident expectation and purpose will cause the universe to move toward you with the right possibilities for your growth. Further, your action, if performed in the light of the intention of harmony and concentration, will bring you continuous, creative opportunity. See the life that you want as if it is pure possibility, and as part of your essence. See yourself in possession of the life and abilities that you so desire. Make use of them in your imagination as if they are your present reality. Meditate upon your purpose and vision until it is clear and distinct, and then take the mental attitude of ownership toward everything in that picture. Take possession of success in your mind, in the full belief that it is truly yours. Hold to this vision and do not waver in your belief that what you desire is yours in heart and mind. Remember to be thankful for blessings received and new inspiration "at all times," as you would when it has taken form. If we can thank the universe for what is imagined in the mind, we will have prosperity and peace, and we will become co-creators of everything that we earnestly want.

Remaining contemplative in action is also part of being in the moment. Your awareness is your "Life Force Consciousness." With focus and refinement of mind, your awakeness will be natural and potent. You will see and sense new ideas and feel the power of intuition and knowingness. You will recognize when to act and how to act, and you will be in tune with the infinite.

2. Higher Purpose in the World

Everyone should engage in a career and occupation that he or she enjoys in a spiritual and productive way. All persons can follow their dreams and exercise their God-given talents in a way that naturally expresses their life force. Therefore, we should be able to feel proud of our work while being rewarded for what we have created and produced for others. This is the law of compensation and flow; a higher purpose involves win-win relationships in which everyone benefits. Our work can be for the good of all those involved, where everyone gets some kind of increase in their lives due to operating with higher purpose. Before becoming fearful of ambition, realize that poverty, misery and sacrifice are not pleasing to anyone. Ambition is merely a desire to adapt, grow and create. In contrast, pretending to be poor, charitable or miserable to achieve attention is a losing proposition. Remember that extreme altruism is no better and no nobler than extreme selfishness, where both are forms of greed. Thus, we can and must believe in the possibility of growth, wealth, and prosperity. As such, we do not have to entertain the idea of scarcity or competition. To achieve abundance, we must create and innovate and we must become who we are supposed to be, and there is no need to compete for the little scraps of food from the table when abundance is plentiful. You know people who work in a field of joy who prosper, and you can do this also. You do not have to take anything from anyone. You do not have to cheat, steal or take advantage in negotiations. You can operate from a win-win perspective where all benefit from your contributions. You must become a creator, not a competitor, and you will get what you want, but in such a way that each person will have more because of your actions.

3. Specificity of Vision & Contemplation

Contemplation of your intentions is similar to planting the seed of your vision or purpose. If we are definite in our intentions and purpose, our dreams can unfold along the lines of our true path. Writing down our intentions is also magical, and has a superb effect, especially in clarifying our direction and goals to ourselves and upon our subconscious mind. However, it is in our mindset that we cultivate what we really want. In order to concentrate our consciousness toward any direction, we must "focus relentlessly during all hours." This means holding constant attention to your vision, with the intent to cause the transformation of your ideas into physical form. We can operate on a plane of mental harmony and good will, and we can flow constructively with life. It is better not to resist potentiality. We can allow life to unfold in conjunction with our constructive and faithful action. We can make the best of ourselves while in a state of peace and well-being. Our highest truth is harmony, bliss, health and success.

4. Strategic Communication

Strategic communication means the way you talk to others and to yourself. Train yourself to think and speak of life getting better and better with unlimited supply. Always speak in terms of forward movement; to do otherwise is to deny your faith.

Safeguard your communications both internally and externally. We should NOT speak of ourselves or our affairs unless with confidants who desire success for us. Never talk about life, career or the economy as sad, or business conditions as terrible. Times may be hard, but business is only bad for those who are operating with a scarcity consciousness.

Remember, you are a constructive creator, your ideas help people, your ideas do not take away from anyone, you can create what you want and you are above fear. When others are having hard times and poor business, you will find your greatest opportunities.

5. Bold, Efficient Action

Every action that we take is either productive or ineffective. Each inefficient action is nonproductive, and if you spend your life doing inefficient things, you will not enjoy peace or success. The more wasteful things that you do, the worse for you. On the other hand, if your every action is constructive, and if every act of your life is efficient, then your whole life will be successful. The causation of failures is doing things in an inefficient manner without focus, and not doing enough things in an efficient manner. You will see that it is a self-evident proposition that if you avoid inefficient acts, and if you do a sufficient number of constructive acts each day, you will enjoy a richer and fuller life.

Every action that is backed by an earnest desire must be strong. Every act can be made strong by contemplating or knowing your purpose while you are doing it. If you also put all the power of love, faith, and gratitude in your action, it can further magnify your power and focus. Ultimately, we must create the means to capture, receive and harvest the fruits that life offers to us so that we can use it for our development and also help mankind. While these steps force creation into motion, your desires may not appear according to your specific wants, but rather manifest in a greater or more appropriate outcome at a later date. Never allow yourself to feel disappointed if this is the case. You can expect to have a certain thing at a certain time, but not get it at that time, and it will appear as a loss. However, if you hold to your faith, you will find that the failure is only temporary. It may be a lesson to take a fresh path. If you do not receive the desired outcome, you may soon get something much better, and you will see that the apparent loss was really a great success.

6. Harmonious Mind

Mindfulness is the controlled and perfected faculty of cognition. It is the mental ability to see beyond what is apparent with clear consciousness. To do this, you must acquire the ability to think the way you want to think. This is the first step toward achieving abundance. Thinking what you want to think is controlling your mental imagery and inner voice, which is enabling truth regardless of appearances. Every person has the natural and inherent power to think what he or she wants to think with practice. Seeing past what seems evident is possible if you are willing to train yourself and allow yourself to grow on a spiritual and metaphysical level. The more you can harmoniously focus your mind while imagining all of your goal's details, the better. This will bring the Supreme Force into accord with your highest good where the universe must cooperate with you. Mental harmony also implies that we should be aware that others on this earth are here to help us and may offer assistance. We should be in tune with these opportunities that may come from many places in the form of other people seeking us out. Harmony is achieved and cultivated by keeping your mind clear of confusion, where it has room to allow flow and goodness to freely enter.

7. Effective Comprehension – Understanding

Effective comprehension means seeing, understanding, interpreting and believing the highest truth. At our lowest level of existence, we see all things as misery and suffering. We can achieve a higher order of living if we can see life as a miracle and go beyond what the critical mind can see. Having the correct view provides peace of mind, the ability to act, the enhanced possibility of good fortune, and a sense of well-being. In the same vein, we manifest internally and externally the thoughts that we have throughout the day, so our views and how we focus our attention are extremely important. Thinking ideas of abundance, health, love, and so on, is a force much greater than any negativity. Sometimes, the correct interpretation of our next move is simply doing what is ahead of us, one thing at a time, with excellence, and doing things right the first time. For higher understanding, we develop a state of mind that is conducive to our desires. We direct positive thoughts, enthusiasm, belief and persistence to be built on truth. Truth can be perceived in a constructive way or we can base our truth on lack or negativity. We all know that a bitter and negative attitude is not an effective way to live and can actually program a person for failure. As they say, "Realists Expect Failure, and Demand to Be Right." Seeing constructive potentiality takes skill and practice. When exercising the principles of a comprehensive awareness, you will expand this skill over time.

8. Joyful Effort

Having a sense of flow with your work and endeavors can be seen as a reward from utilizing a combination of the principles of the 12-fold path. Nothing can be achieved without effort, which is in itself an act of will; whereas, non-definite effort distracts the mind from its task, and confusion may be the consequence. Thus, you must really desire prosperity in your work life. This, in effect, can be compared to detached but focused activity, where you are flowing with the universe with nonresistance of mind.

The clearer and more definite you see yourself in flow and success, the stronger your effort will become, and as your power grows stronger, the easier it will be to hold your mental energy fixed upon the outcome for which you yearn. Behind your earnest and specific vision must be the essence to realize and recognize it to bring it into corporeal expression. Right efforts mixed with confident expectation or faith will become natural productivity animated with results. Behind this intention must be an invincible and unwavering belief that the reward is already yours and that you already have it in possession in your mind's eye. Thus, you need only to take ownership of it psychologically and accept it with an open mind. Live in the new objective, mentally, until it takes form around you physically. No haste is required. However, we know energy is more effective with preparedness. Even the mighty Lincoln said that if he had eight hours to cut down a tree, he would spend six sharpening the axe. Thus, being ready in your mind, body and spirit can enable a seamless flow of action. In the mental realm, enter into full enjoyment of the things you want. "Whatsoever things ye ask for when ye pray, believe that ye receive them, and ye shall have them," said The Great Master.

9. Open to Receive Inspiration

Many people from around the world feel unworthy of abundance. Many do not value themselves, their abilities, their talents or their work. It is very important to learn to feel worthy and deserving of good. You are a unique and spiritual being created by the universe with a celestial purpose. As a unique being in communion with the universal flow of ideas, you should become mentally open to receiving all good things in life. Further, people should be careful to allow the receipt of blessings into their lives from the universe and from others. *Example:* Accepting a compliment from another person or having a method of being rewarded financially.

True and lasting prosperity has a spiritual foundation that includes balance. Successful persons master excellence in body, mind and spirit. When there is balance, ideas and energy flow from the universe to the person who is exercising this higher realm of existence. When we are at our best and acting as spiritually effective individuals, we actually have more ideas flowing to us from the "universal mind" or consciousness of the infinite.

Therefore, we can participate in our destiny and co-create our own reality. If you read the great spiritual minds of the Renaissance, you will quickly see that it is the right of the individual to have a direct experience with the Deity of your understanding through prayer, meditation and getting back to the spiritual basics. Taking quiet time to meditate, pray or contemplate may indeed create an untold mystical flow of inspiration to all who try.

10. Gratitude and Belief – The Vibration

Gratitude and thankfulness lead to greater constructive expectation in our daily living. Positive expectation and confident expectation that is based in belief IS THE SUBSTANCE OF FAITH.

Recognize possibility, praise others, bless others, and bless and praise yourself. Blended with humility, your harmonious connection to a universal spirit will allow a pipeline of grace to flow upon you. A thankful heart is highly conducive to faith, bliss and living with joy. Realize that you are free to create abundance and that you are worthy of the gifts of the universe. With your higher belief, you free your mind's mental and spiritual power to focus on what you want. What you think about becomes expansive in your life. Your focus on the good and the great will bring these miracles into your world.

Faith and belief are the deciding energy in many situations. All things created equal, the scientific probability of a coin toss result is 50 percent in its purest form. However, it only takes a grain of sand to tilt the balance of a scale in one direction. Thus, something as small as a mustard seed on one side of the balance can, in fact, lean the probability of prosperity in one direction versus another. In sum, the cosmic cards can begin to be dealt in your favor with the influence of intention and gratitude. In the end, happiness and gratitude are reasonable options that lead to the greater possibility of success and peace of mind.

11. Love Energy and Forgiveness

Love is the quality of thought and emotion that will propel us into a state of bliss and achievement.

Love all there is. Focus on the good, the great, the constructive and the beauty of life. See the best in all there is. Look for the good that occurs in the world.

Meditate on the people who have been kind to you, the creation all around you, the good that happens every day, the inventions for the betterment of humanity and the positive happenings around the world that occur each and every day. Learn to love all and love yourself, and love will be attracted to you. Love is a composite of many things including gratitude, harmlessness, peace, kindness and compassion. Thinking love and giving love will liberate you into the fourth dimension of harmony. Think of how you have already been blessed, protected, and guided throughout your life. Yes, lessons have been learned, and further happiness, peace and success may be yours if you stay on the path of quantum bliss.

Cultivating love and forgiveness can dispel otherwise discouraging thoughts. Great minds can look back on things they love or have loved, and they can recapture that emotion at any moment. Your dreams will be realized as long as you do not resist the gifts of abundance and remain aware of life's gifts.

Contemplate the concepts of St. Paul: Patience, Kindness, Understanding, Generosity, Sincerity, Humility, Gentleness… Love never fails.

12. Wisdom – Having these qualities: Experience, Knowledge & Perception

Wisdom is said to be composed of the qualities of experience, knowledge and good judgment. Acting with wisdom is said to be the path of prosperity. Having money, good looks or power is not necessary, but having wisdom is a requirement for health, happiness and success. As they say, a man with money meets a man with experience, and the man with the money gets an experience, while the man with experience ends up with the money.

Having the power to picture potential and make healthy decisions and winning choices will create a life of prosperity and abundance. While wisdom is crucial, acting upon it is also the mother of the greatest successes in history.

*These concepts from *The 12-Fold Path* are inspired by the combined teachings of many great masters, including Pythagoras, Marcus Aurelius, Schopenhauer, Hegel, Swedenborg, Emerson, Napoleon Hill, William Walker Atkinson, Charles Haanel, Genevieve Behrend, Epicurean Thought, Stoicism, Taoism, Confucianism, Thoreau, and W. Wattles. Everything is possible with desire, faith, love, harmonious action and constructive thinking. Remember that these are important steps in our pursuit of excellence and peace. Take the best ideas from the list and use them to improve your life.

Chapter 5

Spiritual and Success Exercises

1. Visualize Your Day – At night, review your day hour by hour. Try to remember what you did from the time you woke up to the end of the day. See each event, each interaction, each relationship. After this visualization, consider the things that you could have done better. With this precept of order, much like the spiritual exercises of Ben Franklin over 200 years ago, you may build your character as well as your imagination skills each day.

2. Contemplative Prayer – Prayer, breath work, meditation, visualization and recognition of health and peace can be taken point by point through the body using a quasi-chakra observance system. When doing the health exercises in this book, take care to also imagine a healing light going through each chakra region.

Exercise: Sit in a chair or lie down. Close your eyes. Take in air through your nose, hold it for seven seconds, and then let it out of your mouth slowly. Do this at least three times to enter a relaxed state. Clench your fists and then extend your fingers as far as they will go. Repeat a few times and then put your hands in your lap. Now clear your mind and imagine a peaceful scene such as a mountain meadow with flowers or a calm lake. Begin with either the top of your head or the base or lower body. Go through each of the seven sections in one direction. The first letters of the colors are "ROY G BIV" (red, orange, yellow, green, blue, indigo, violet) with red beginning with the lower body and the head/crown corresponding to the color violet.

Now, go through all seven colors one by one, imagining the color of each chakra and the corresponding section of the body. Imagine each color purifying and regenerating the body, one by one. Relax and purify each section of the body as you go. When you have finished the exercise from head to lower body, or lower body to head, release any impure energy to the universe while taking a few breaths from the nose and blowing out from the mouth. Then, express a mental thanks to the Supreme Power for the healing energy. Open your eyes.

1. Muladhara (Sanskrit: Mūlādhāra) – Color: Red; Lower body – our connection to the earth and the physical plane – Survival and Operation
2. Svadhisthana (Sanskrit: Svādhisthāna) – Color: Orange; Reproductive gland region of the body – our creative and procreative urges and drives
3. Manipura (Sanskrit: Manipūra) – Color: Yellow; Stomach/navel – energy center for power and manifestation and desires (location: solar plexus)
4. Anahata (Sanskrit: Anāhata) – Color: Green; Heart – energy center for love
5. Vishuddha (Sanskrit: Viśuddha) – Color: Blue; Throat – center for expression
6. Ajna (Sanskrit: Ājñā) – Color: Indigo; Eyebrow or forehead between brows – our psychic powers
7. Sahasrara (Sanskrit: Sahasrāra) – Color: Violet; Top of head and crown – connection with the Cosmic or the divine

3. Breathing and Purification – Try to learn the purification breath work. Breathe slowly into your nose and out from your mouth. Imagine negative energy leaving your body with each exhale and see yourself with each intake breath taking in life, love, pure energy and healing elements.

4. Sensory Perception – Learn to feel each part of the body uniquely. Sit or lie down and close your eyes. Then, pick a part of your body. Sense it, feel it, imagine where it is. If a part of your body has aches, pains or dis-ease, then use this exercise to send healing energy to that spot in a targeted way.

5. Constructive Journaling – Every month or every three to six months, sit down and write out things that you are proud of. Write 10 things that you have done to improve your life in recent months. List your best attributes. Write out 5–10 things that you enjoy doing or would like to try. List things that you can do to respect yourself. Even write out a few luxury to-dos where you can take action each year to treat yourself to a trip, family fun, to luxury or to learning.

6. COT: Cognitive Occupational Therapy – Every few days or weeks, you must do things that are cognitive and that involve neuroplasticity exercises. Examples include: learning to recite a poem or prayer, working puzzles, crosswords or even chores such as unloading the dishwasher, building a model, writing a story, telling a story, preparing and giving a presentation or related activities. The "mind-hand" or "mind-speech" activity is very stimulating and builds mental muscle.

7. Vibration – Your vibration can be at many levels. To say the least, you can enhance your mental vibration through various actions. Higher levels of mental and spiritual vibrations include Love, Gratitude, Praise, Faith, Feel Good Emotions and more. Many practitioners work on a daily basis to enhance and bring their mental and spiritual vibration to a higher level. Practitioners do this so that they may lead a more harmonious life, but also to attract people, events and things of the same or higher vibration. The end result of healthy vibrations is the attraction of more constructive events, outcomes and possibilities.

8. Euphoric Modeling – Recall a certain past event or image that brings feelings of joy, happiness, peace, love or endearment. Have this MOMENT at your beck and call. Whenever you feel a pestering negative thought, seize upon the moment of peace and seek out solutions, forgiveness and peace of mind.

9. Cause and Effect – For every thought, action or inaction, there is a corresponding thought and event. Your heartfelt emotions, when mixed with constructive thought and action, carry more force than the average thought and action. Building a foundation is vital to this step. At first, we must change our mentality from one of lack to a consciousness and mind of possibility. Our minds and hearts evolve and begin to believe in opportunity and abundance. Instead of thinking why, we transcend to a spiritual position of why not. At this juncture, we begin to take action in accordance with our dreams. Each mental and physical action we take on a daily basis adds to the momentum of our spiritual force. Our spiritual force in conjunction with our harmonious and constructive thinking begins to manifest higher realities in our days to come.

10. Habits and Routines – Develop healthier routines by seeking out activities that build your life and improve your circumstances. Learn to reward yourself for superior habits. Sit down with a trusted advisor and analyze your daily routines. Review your rituals, what you watch, how you exercise, how you think, where you go, who you associate with, and what you do to respect yourself. Evaluate all of these things and then determine how to better treat yourself to a life of excellence, self-regard, transformation and fewer distractions.

Chapter 6

Concise Laws of Success

Key Metaphysical Laws and Philosophical Concepts

The Law of Cooperation

We must learn to cooperate with Spirit. We, as students of metaphysics, realize that a harmonious relationship with our spiritual self creates a relationship of peace and success. We must clear ourselves mentally to create room for harmony and peace that fill our souls with constructive spirit energy. Then, we must develop a consciousness of cooperation, flow and unity with Spirit.

The Law of Modeling

Our external environment and our spiritual and physical interactions are important. If we associate with like minds of a spiritual nature who desire success, we can excel quickly. By seeking wisdom, we find insight and learn to be the best by learning from the best. Seek the company of those who are constructive. Project and act out the ideal image of yourself. Learn to reinvent yourself and grow toward your desired character. Avoid people who are destructive in their speech, mind and actions. You should cultivate the most spiritual and healthy mental states. Engage life, stay active and help others, and other people will help you in turn.

The Law of Thought Energy

We think, therefore, we create. We are builders of thoughts and ideas; what you think is radiated outward. Your thoughts attract like thoughts. Through constructive thinking, focus, concentration, action, gratitude, thanksgiving and praise, positive outcomes will be brought to you. Be very specific in your creative visualization and desires. You are a magnet for higher good if you nurture an attitude of harmony and abundance.

The Law of Intention
The courage to think what you want and to take action toward your objectives is the ultimate power. This ability may allow you to see in your mind's eye what it is you want and will do. This type of visualization and mental planning prepares you for each day's actions and work. In the present moment, we must do all we can toward our objectives. We cannot change yesterday or do tomorrow's work; we must use our mind and actions toward today's tasks and mission.

The Law of Love Energy
Love is the quality of thought and emotion that will propel us into peace of mind and great success. Love all there is. Think about the people who have been kind to you, the creation all around you, the good that happens, the inventions for the betterment of humanity and the positive happenings around the world that occur every day. Learn to love all and love yourself, and then love will be attracted to you. Love is a form of gratitude, harmlessness, peace, kindness and compassion. Thinking love and giving love will liberate you into the fourth dimension of thought. Think of how you have been blessed, protected and guided throughout your life.

The Law of Optimum Ideas and Opulence
Thoughts of the best, thoughts of health, thoughts of harmonious relationships, thoughts of peace and thoughts of wealth will project into the world and mold your destiny. Health, beauty, confidence and success are mostly a state of mind. For example, we have all seen average-looking superstars be regarded as beautiful. Thus, how we think and carry ourselves most

definitely affects how we are perceived and how we feel from day to day.

The Law of Authenticity

To engage in life and head toward our true purpose is fundamentally important. People who relegate themselves to something that they do not want to do for their lifetimes are inhibiting their happiness and their potential service to humanity. The abundance of the world effectively provides for all of us in many ways. Each person must seek out what he or she wants from life, knowing that what is needed will be provided. Nobody is stopping us from following our dreams. We have the ability to consciously think and plan our future, and we have choices and an abundance of opportunity. Ask yourself what you want to be, with whom you want to be, and how and where you want to live. Think about the possibilities, the choices of jobs, careers, business ventures and creative alternatives that you have presently and for the future. Imagine the real freedom that you have right now. Then, envision all of the great gifts and prospects that you have in your life.

The Law of Spiritual Energy

We must learn the effective use of our spiritual and emotional energy. If we live in the past and dwell on wrongs in our lives, then our energy is dissipated in favor of the ills of yesterday. Do not blame your past for anything. You are capable of all things new – your body and mind can be renewed altogether with continued metaphysical focus. If we use our thoughts and visualization toward our desired ideals and mix them with our constructive emotion, then we can move quickly toward what we want from life. Prolonged self-sabotages such as resentment, anger, hatred and self-loathing will indeed inhibit our growth and happiness. Free your mind from self-tyranny by transcending the past, asking for forgiveness, making amends when appropriate, engaging in character development and self-appraisal, and contemplating atonement.

The Law of Creative Source

All things are possible with the source, which works in you and through you. We are all parts of the infinite power, a power ever carrying us up to higher, finer grades of being. Good is on your side; God is your partner in life. Your faith power will be induced through your harmonious and thankful mindset and action. Never underestimate yourself, never speak with discouragement to others and do not keep the habit of doubting opportunity and good.

In Christianity, the Lord has the power to command the elements and quiet the storm. Your spirit, as a part of the great whole, has the same power that is only waiting for fruition within you. Christ revealed through the power of concentrated belief that he could turn that unseen element into the seen, and he could materialize abundance in the form of health, loaves, and fish.

The word "impossible" has limits. Impossible is a typical response by others who may not know the potential of any situation. Thinking that dreams are unattainable is a common excuse to not do anything. Remember to ask yourself: why not do it, or why not try?

The Law of Regeneration

The body has many capabilities: it can grow, heal, renew, learn and do great works. However, we must realize that rest and relaxation are vitally important to this growth and renewal. The body, or temple, is renewing itself daily with new cells, and cleansing itself of the old. When we permit our body and soul to regenerate, it will do so quickly if we maintain spiritual harmony.

The Law of Faith
There are rewards in having belief and a childlike faith This expectant view regards all things as if they are possible; it provides a viable probability of success and happiness. Be open to an inflowing force of abundance. Allow yourself to change for the better, take action and move forward toward your highest good. Remember that success is always a reasonable option through faith.

The Law of Constructive Thought
Begin your day by taming your mind with spiritual and constructive thoughts. Feed your body, mind and soul with the best food, information and spiritual energy. Act, think and be good to yourself and others; ask and petition from your higher power all that you want. Hope and pray for the best to happen to everyone. Bless, praise and be thankful for all things good. Empower yourself and your spirit with love, gratitude, kindness, harmonious thinking, harmless action and serenity. Your needs will be met by the universe as long as you do not resist the gifts of abundance.

The Law of Positive Energy
A new mental energy level is possible. It is a simple adjustment to the way we use our thought. Try not to complain for a whole day. Try to stop blaming, and quit making excuses for not doing what you desire. Your thoughts and character can be reinvented – you can be reborn! Your mind and thinking can transcend into a new constructive awareness. It takes effort, but anyone can do it. We must be persistent. In life or business, we must press on in mind to achieve the successful results that we desire. Each day is a new opportunity to engage in several successful tasks with your higher vibration.

The Law of Focus

Energy should be directed and focused upon what you want to expand in your life. Negative focus can lead to frustration. Therefore, the concentration of your thoughts upon the best and being your best (in mind and action) can lead to a life of harmonious and effective living. Life will become easier when you can flow with it instead of resist it, and thus making an effective use of your decisions, time and energy. Don't worry about what was; instead, focus on what you want to become and how you can help others. Each day, engage in constructive tasks toward your dreams and building high character.

The Law of Spiritual Economy

Economy has been addressed by the greats such as Ben Franklin, and it is documented in the ancient wisdom literature of early cultures. There must be a balance in efficiencies and effectiveness to create the right amount of effort and corresponding results. Make the best of your endeavors and constructively use your assets and talents; there is no need for haste or waste. You can be creative and successful without hurting anyone; you can help many.

The Law of Integrity

Your integrity is part of your character. Character can be developed to provide the positive impression upon all those with whom you meet and interact. Do what you say you will do, and do it right the first time. People will soon recognize that you follow through on your commitments and that you are a person of strength, honesty, power and trust. Further, this habit of following through with your obligations to yourself and others will drive you to be a very successful person. Avoiding things that are not a constructive use of your time will benefit all around you, and you will not engage in actions that do not improve your own life.

The Law of Preparation and Planning

A plan or objective is fundamental to the clarification of your desire. A large majority of people are afraid to specify what they intend to do. Transcending this fear and taking bold action upon your plans and strategies allows for the growth and manifestation of your idea into a reality. Preparing for your goals is fundamental, so plan what you are going to do and be very specific. Outline the steps needed and drive toward the desired outcome. Be prepared for outcomes that are as good as or even better than what you desire. Know what you will do and prepare for any circumstance of importance. Be ready to act, engage, communicate, contemplate and receive your good.

The Law of Empathy

The ability to put yourself in the shoes of another will allow you to develop an understanding of others. We do not always know what other people are thinking or experiencing; thus, we try to understand others' goals and challenges. Let your kindness and gentleness be known. Speak and act with confidence, strength and grace, and do not react to the world. Respond to it with poise and treat others in the ways that you would want to be treated. Learn to communicate and receive opportunities by first understanding what others are saying.

The Law of Sincerity

Honesty is interrelated to truth. There is the truth that others speak, but more importantly, there is the truth of what we perceive and analyze. When we operate on this earthly plane, we must try to view truth at the highest level. If you sincerely act and think in constructive ways, then vast opportunity will be attracted to you as your truth. *Like attracts like*. You need not seek power over others. Give others the impression of increase, and they will be attracted to your value, service, wisdom and the quality of your living. Be earnest in your character.

The Law of Harmonious Relationships

Be connected with all that is good. Keep a harmonious relationship with the world through various strategies. Using gratitude for any of your gifts on a daily basis can grow your expectation of good and faith. It is much easier to be connected when you have set aside or removed destructive thinking, including resentment, jealously and other blocks and barriers.

The Law of Desire

Desires are good and excellent. Desires bring focus on enriching your life and following your true direction. Cultivating desires into reality is vital for change, innovation and improvement. You would not have a desire unless it was possible, but follow through on ideas where you have a solid sphere of possibility. An earnest and heartfelt desire is energized and empowered for success.

The Law of Self-Reliance

You are to become rich in life. Spiritual abundance is yours – it is your birthright. Your sixth sense becomes available to you through your connection to spiritual abundance and prosperity. Your connection and harmony with the universe allows you to cooperate and co-create with the world. You will become self-reliant because you are moving closer to your true place, which is utilizing your unique and creative abilities. Your true place is your right livelihood, your labor of love. Your career and efforts will be further harmonized to become a wealth of opportunity and abundance in your personal and working endeavors. Remain committed to your dreams and your true self so that your given talents will unfold and multiply.

The Law of Having

Mentally seeing and feeling the outcome or result as if you have it already is very important. It allows you to see the rewards, and it further facilitates feelings surrounding the outcome. Harvesting positive feelings about the outcome is very important to energize a desire, mission, visualization and result. Have what you want in your mind and allow it to materialize.

The Law of Vision and Mission
A vision is important in that you clarify the results of your long-term goals and your destination. A mission is important in that you can quantify and clarify the means that will be used to achieve the desired future outcome, which is part of the journey.

The Law of Visualization and Imagination
Mental visualization of your objectives holds great importance. Seeing what you intend to do as if it is reality is a powerful mental exercise that is vital to the codification and building of the objective so as to assist the manifestation of the result. Seeing exactly what you desire and intend causes you to specify your wants and desires. The stronger and longer you can hold your ideal in your mind's eye, the better.

The Law of Efficiency
Pointing your mental faculties toward the individual actions required to achieve a task, project or goal results in effectiveness – as long as your acts are efficient. Continuous and persistent thinking and action toward your work, goal, project or desired outcome can funnel or intensify the energy in a specific direction. Completion and finalization of acts and tasks, one by one and in a successful manner, create momentum toward an objective.

The Law of Boldness
Boldness and action create the spark that energizes an idea. Boldness is what may cause opportunity, serendipity of events and is what will draw people to be attracted to you. Therefore, contemplation mixed with action is the optimal, blended solution.

The Law of Cause and Effect

Every action has a reaction. Types of actions and thoughts attract similar actions and thoughts. Kindness tends to bring kindness; respect tends to bring respect. Additionally, constructive thinking tends to bring constructive opportunities and events to the individual.

The Law of Increase

All mankind tends to be attracted to those who can bring more life or enrichment. If an individual projects life and opportunity, then he or she will attract similar minds.

The Law of Seeking Wisdom

Wisdom is the ability to think something over, discuss it with others or seek out counsel from those who understand or know the subject well. Thus, the use of lessons learned and opinions of experts is a valid consideration in thinking and acting.

The Law of Love, Forgiveness and Harmony

Cultivating love and forgiveness can dispel otherwise destructive thoughts. Great minds can look back on things they love or have loved, and they can re-harness that emotion at will. This power is essential to continuing your path of positivity and growth.

The Law of Self-Regard

There is something very real in taking care of yourself and your affairs, and in minding your own business. Your enhanced mind, body, soul and financial affairs allow you to help those you love, and you can serve humanity in better ways. The greatest way to be of service to your loved ones is to make the best of yourself.

The Law of Gratitude

A sincere, heartfelt gratitude for life and its gifts will allow the flow of good to you. Systematic recognition of people or things to be thankful for may facilitate an expectation of good and growth of inherent faith. Integrating this confident expectation with your aspirations creates great power.

The Law of Response-Ability

Speaking of only positive things can attract opportunity and friends. Guarded speech can protect you from negative forces. Keeping your desires and goals close to you will keep the energy of the new ideas from becoming dissipated. Sharing your desires and goals with those who support, encourage and assist you can be a constructive exercise and can help harvest constructive feedback. Be sure to focus communication with those who will support you, in order to prevent negative force on your thoughts.

The Law of Creativity

Your creative power IS your wealth. This gift is pure and free. Your mind allows you to develop ideas with *no* limits. Less educated people believe that competition causes a limited supply of creation and ideas. However, creativity always manifests abundance for all. As an example, an individual who creates a new cure to solve a health problem is not competing against the world, but is instead helping it.

The Law of Right Livelihood

Having a labor of love can cause effectiveness and efficiency through enthusiastic work. Doing something that you believe in or selling a product that you have faith in can make any job much easier or even fun. Having fun with work is a divine right.

The Law of Blessing and Expansion

People seem to enjoy a greater state of well-being and success when they bless their relationship with the universe, bless their loved ones, bless their home and give thanks for their health on a daily basis.

The Law of Detachment

When we become too attached or dependent on a potential result, we limit ourselves from the gifts of the universe. It is good to expect the best, but it is also smart to allow for something better to unfold. Thus, trying to control a specific outcome without any flexibility can inhibit the universe from its creativity.

The Law of Receiving

Many people from around the world feel unworthy of abundance, not valuing themselves, their service, their talents or work. It is very important to learn to feel worthy, unique and deserving of good. Moreover, you should become mentally open to receiving all good things in life. People should be careful to create ways to receive the good into their lives from the universe and from others, such as accepting a compliment from another person.

The Law of Like Minds

When you engage a mentality of abundance and harmonious spiritual thinking, your mind will expand and increase when radiating love, prosperity and health. Thus, your powers of attraction will increase. The universe will send people to help you; it will be your job to select and allow them to assist you in a win-win relationship to expand your abundance where all can achieve a richer and fuller life through these ventures.

The Law of Resistance

Types of resistance that inhibit your abundance, health and connection with the spirit are resentment, jealousy, anger, judgment, criticism, hatred, greed, pride and mental laziness. Other subtle resistance occurs when faced with change. It is better to adapt than to perish, while maintaining your unique qualities.

The Law of Willingness
Willingness is the key to advancement. Be willing to take action, take a chance or risk failure or embarrassment. Without willingness, you may never engage mental, spiritual or physical action that leads to good. Willingness is a vital ingredient toward successful visualization, belief, action, planning and success. Ask yourself, "Am I willing to believe, to try, to engage? Can it be done? Why or why not?"

The Law of Inventory
Holding onto old, counterproductive ideas and unneeded things can keep you from growth, spiritual flow and expansion. You should take an inventory of mental ideas and material things and eliminate those that create inconvenience, frustration, clutter and resentment to allow freedom and harmony in your life. When you prune the tree, it allows for new growth; when you clear out your mind, it creates space for more good.

The Law of Causation
Root out the cause of your failures, your inconveniences, your frustration and your mental or spiritual disabilities. If you have a problem, there may be a cause. If you injured yourself engaging in a specific activity, you may avoid this activity in the future, or you can better prepare for it next time. Otherwise, you may pay for this repeated action in the form of more pain and suffering. If you have a relationship that always seems to leave you in pain, then you may need to avoid this person if you are spiritually whole and they are not.

The Law of Forgiveness and Karma
You may feel you have wronged many people. You may even feel guilty for past deeds or encounters. However, if you feel remorse and intend to act as a better person from now on, then you have made progress. In any event, your day-to-day action and

character of goodness and kindness will build your positive energy where the world will protect you and serve you.

The Law of Humility

Keep an open mind and keep faith in the universe. Put your spirit before ego. Meek is not weak – it is strong, confident, cooperative and advantageous. Developing an honest appraisal of yourself can be healthy. You can always improve yourself, your credentials, your relationships and your business. When somebody has hurt your feelings, said you were wrong, said no to you or otherwise attacked you, it is best to analyze when possible and discuss the issue with another supportive person before retaliating.

The Law of Purity

Peace allows growth and focus. Clarity and concentration are primary keys to serenity. Being able to operate on a plane with singleness of mind can allow you to achieve great things. A person who cannot focus and achieve one thing at a time may never cross the finish line with any dream, goal or aspiration. Overall, if you allow resentment, frustration, hate of another or fear to dominate your thoughts, then your effectiveness will be diminished. Hard work is required to keep you focused on bettering yourself. Overall, your freedom, vitality and wholeness depend on your effectiveness.

The Law of Balance

Enough emphasis cannot be put on the necessary balance between body, mind and spirit. It sounds easy, but all people need to honor their bodies, improve their minds and evolve their spiritual nature. Many organizations emphasize that when you are out of balance, you have placed too much energy and focus in only one area of your life. For example, you can work or exercise too much, both of which can harm your immune system, muscles and daily regeneration process.

The Law of Visual Affirmation

If you cannot paint the mental picture as clearly as you want, then try to use the material world to enhance your mind. Cut out pictures from magazines or books of the ideal things you want, and assemble them into a collage or on poster board. Rip out images of the home you desire, people having fun, distant places that you want to visit or the lifestyle and types of relationships that you desire. This action can help you amalgamate the images to imprint them on your subconscious mind. View them daily and place them in a prominent place. Overall, imagine having these attributes or things in your quiet time. Sense the joy of living your dreams.

The Law of Atonement

For thousands of years, mystical and spiritual organizations have encouraged self-analysis, confession, atonement and even restitution. This spiritual housecleaning can free the mind from guilt, shame and even self-defeating thoughts. Forgiveness of others and the forgiveness of self is a very important process for self-actualization and personal effectiveness.

The Law of Pruning

The continuous development of character means letting go of habits that are not working for you anymore. When you prune the tree of dead branches, you make room for new growth.

The Law of Peace of Mind

Peace of mind transcends all material desires. Most philosophers define happiness as peace of mind. As we know, each of us has our own subjective version of what peace of mind would be; however, this peace would of course imply faith and a freedom from pain, ignorance, worry, mental misery and self-destructive thoughts. Further, peace of mind is obtained by self-actualization.

The Law of Opulence

Wealth and opulence are keenly tied to worthiness. Sometimes our minds are too wrapped up in hoarding and therefore not circulating our abundance. Thus, it is sometimes good to simply act as if you were rich, and play the part. At other times, it is best to treat yourself to something that you deserve, such as a vacation, new car, massage, hobby enhancement, clothes, ideal home or tools for effective work. When you begin to respect yourself in a greater fashion, your body responds – and the world also responds.

The Law of Power

Mental strength is something earned. It takes willingness and effort to obtain potency. When we intentionally grow our latent powers, we are able to meet opportunities or challenges with preparedness.

The Law of Courage

Courage is better than cowardice. Examples of courage include acting with boldness to help others, or even simply stepping up to your responsibilities. In today's world, perseverance implies taking action and not procrastinating. Without action, an idea cannot begin initial movement or obtain energy that it needs to manifest.

The Law of Affirmations and Meditations

It can be argued that many people are best served by learning to become silent and open to the universe. I believe that there are two types of affirmative personalities. One personality is best served with quiet communion with its higher self. The other is best served with affirmations and prayers that assist in changing their thoughts. One is active and the other is passive. A combination of both would be excellent, but many people focus on one system at a time.

The Law of Seeking
Life is growth and is a series of changes. Being prepared for change is the key to peaceful transition. We should be continuously seeking life, spirit and growth.

The Law of Natural Expression
When you reach periods in your life when you are truly happy, it is probably because you are expressing yourself naturally on a level of spirit, relationships, creation and livelihood.

The Law of Infinite Growth
The world is overflowing with supply. As an example, the birds of the world can adapt, migrate, grow and provide for themselves. There is a never-ending quantity of material and substance to create what is needed on this earth. If something ever becomes scarce, a more efficient substitute is prepared or invented. Ideas, creativity and imagination have solved millions of challenges in just our lifetime alone. The universe is in a constant state of building, innovating, expanding and creating, and we have the power to be part of that.

The Law of Change
Getting out of your comfort zone and taking some small action in the direction of your needs, wants or desires can sometimes be the spark of creation. This spark can often create a whirlwind of activities, insights, ideas and help from others.

The Law of Magnetism
As for charismatic energy, the great American author Napoleon Hill implies that we all have many forms of inner energy, which include our forces of magnetism and attraction, or sexual energy. Hill's years of research on the most successful people revealed this astounding secret. Thus, concentration is critical to focus all forms of your inner energy toward your goals, influence, leadership and

desires. If you are focusing your primary energies in scattered areas, you are in essence diffusing your power instead of harnessing it toward your goal. To prevent distraction, a practitioner must be able to transmute and direct all of his or her mental, spiritual, physical and charismatic energy.

The Law of Vibration
Feeling grateful and focusing on thankfulness will invariably change your thinking, your vibration and how you react to life. It will also charge your spirit with hope and the expectation of faith and opportunities.

The Law of Living in the Now
We must not live in the past or future. Sooner or later, we must learn when to work, and when to enjoy life in its purest form. Find out what you love to do, master yourself and then learn to both live and relax.

The Law of Honor
What is honor? Being honorable involves your thoughts, words and deeds. An honorable person is a person of belief, service and charity whose self-control transcends all drama and hostility.

The Law of Individualism
Freedom is better than servitude. We must learn to break free of overdependence or being tied down to anything that can cause injury over the long-term. We must make the best of ourselves from a standpoint of mind, education, health, body, spirit and harmony. We become free to express ourselves naturally and effectively. Further, it is better not to interfere with others in their natural hunger to learn, grow, earn, succeed and work.

The Law of Hospitality and Kinship
Hospitality is a word that implies helping our brothers and

sisters. What is key to the concept of hospitality is loving our neighbors; hospitality and kinship are better than alienation. By helping those who want to help themselves and by being of service to those who can't, we open the door for the universe to shower us with continued opportunity and gifts.

The Law of Appearance
What is the truth? Do we know the facts? Should we try to learn more? Do we have time to investigate? Do we need to take action? Is the meaning that we have attached to the truth constructive or simply based on ego or the delusional mind?

The Law of Vigor
Industriousness is better than lifelessness. As we know, doing two or three things per day effectively can create massive progress during a lifetime. If we can help ourselves and help others, our family and community also benefit and excel.

The Law of Giving and Tithing
Taking time to give money, service or goods to divine recipients will create untold flow in your life. Life requires circulation of your ideas, your things and your service. It is virtually guaranteed that your existence will be blessed and protected through your giving of yourself. You are not doing this to take advantage of the law – you do this to expand your spiritual way of life, keep the flow and give back. Expecting something in return is not necessary because the universe will provide opportunity for you by your embracing this process.

The Law of Fidelity
Principles are better than universalism. Being true to yourself and following your dreams leads to your happiness. We are all unique. We must make decisions, take positions and take action. Sometimes we must choose sides. With that being said, we must

be strategic with our decisions while also trying to intelligently foresee the consequences of each of our individual decisions. We should help those who are open to suggestion and seek to better themselves in an effort to become self-reliant and productive.

Chapter 7

Summary of Spiritual Empowerment

The Steps to Obtain Freedom, Peace and Wealth

1. As beings that desire increasing life, we each contain energies of body, mind and spirit, and we must maintain equilibrium between all three energies. To preserve this balance, we utilize our threefold powers. Use of mental, spiritual and physical powers in a spiritual way must produce abundance.

2. All thoughts begin with an idea, which is the byproduct of divine connection to the source of all thought.

3. The ideas behind the thoughts are the mystical form of all creation and the underpinnings of tangible results or manifestation.

4. All thoughts tend to lead to the field of potential outcomes for all actions, inactions and creation.

5. Deep thinking or what is believed in the mind habitually becomes who you are, and is your essence or character.

6. Free will creates choices for which commitments must be selected. We all have the ability to choose how we use our free will in terms of thoughts and actions.

7. Choices create the nucleus of new form and begin a chain reaction if the choice is fueled with emotion and belief.

8. Emotions that fuel manifestation are love, joy, peace, happiness, goodness and other positive emotions.

9. When each idea is transformed into an intention, then each intention may be transformed into a plan, vision and mission. After this, it is then chosen as a prime objective for the individual.

10. When the plan becomes your dominant thought, it

becomes a purpose that is backed by belief.

11. When firm belief, earnestness and constructive emotion back up a purpose, it is energized.

12. Our belief system must be based on the constant and creative possibility of optimal results and prosperity. Everyone who is living upright in a spiritual way is deserving and capable of tapping into this abundance.

13. We become best at co-creating our destiny when we are in spiritual unity with the universe, when a person develops the realization of the Divine Presence within one's own self.

14. We operate most effectively when we are awakened and clear in mind. Attunement and forgiveness of ourselves and others allows us to be free of anger and to live in the present moment fully in an awakened state of mind.

15. For acceptance, we must believe that prosperity and well-being is our birthright.

16. Believe that you have wealth and freedom and that you are the essence of creative ability.

17. Everything that is needed is continually provided by an ever-expanding world and universe that is abundant and impersonal.

18. We must understand the essence or rationale behind the purpose of each desire that we want to cultivate.

19. Further, we must comprehend in some way how our big ideas will help others along with ourselves to convey the sincere impression of value, worth and increase.

20. Before implementing each plan or taking any big step, we evaluate our mental effectiveness, getting clear and going through a catharsis of mind. This means looking at your track record, atone, prune, purge and clear away the mental debris. Begin to use "what works" and start to utilize the best practices that make you efficient.

21. Have clear objectives. Set specific goals, then research

and refine them. After the purpose, task and objective are clear, then push forward with persistence.

22. Be results-driven in everything you plan. What is the mission, destination and vision? Develop affirmations that correlate to the most favorable end result.

23. Think, feel and act "AS IF" you are already in possession of the life that you want. Cultivate your emotions and your character around the "As If." You must become what you want, which means you become the person who owns the life you desire.

24. Look at where you are and where you are going, and periodically reset the course and navigation to optimize the journey.

25. Learn to think and speak in a prosperous way that conveys peace, abundance and increase. Mold the habits and tendencies of your thought. Refuse to accept lack and fear.

26. Take action. Keep lists and do three things toward your dreams per day, and do them constructively to the best of your ability.

27. Study your life, reflect on your day and decide how to continually improve yourself. Do your homework and do all you can to learn and know your purpose, your objectives and how to master your skills. Be the best at what you do and BE KNOWN for your excellence.

28. Practice meditation and prayer. Write out affirmative meditations such as, "Each day I am improving." Write out 10 statements that are affirming and positive. Contemplate over them each day. You can write out generalized affirmations or very specific ones.

29. Use the affirmative statements or contemplation to increase acceptance of your potential and boost your awareness.

30. Visualize – See yourself in optimal circumstances in your mind's eye and then feel it. If you can visualize the optimal

result, then see the next step. Example: see yourself a few pounds leaner toward your optimal weight.

31. Choose your environment. Select what to feed yourself. Mold your circumstances by your actions and specific thoughts.

32. Organize your affairs. Gain the habit of finishing things well. Become excellent, simplify your life, empty the clutter and redefine your focus. Develop prosperity-based routines.

33. Imprint and affirm your ideals and dreams into your consciousness. The plan, desired thing, or result must be written down and then verbalized. It should be claimed into this world using the spoken word.

34. Make wealth and excellence a priority. Align your thoughts to attract excellence and wealth. Be aware, be open, learn to receive from others, offer praise and appreciate life. Accept your potentiality, gifts and abundance.

35. Circulate your GOOD. Donate time or money to people or organizations that are the source of your spiritual sustenance.

36. Develop your sixth sense. Learn and practice creativity, awareness and contemplation. Keep a journal, write out ideas, develop and allow a universal flow of inspiration and ideas into your life.

37. Review and remember your actions. Reflect on what you have done well each day and the things in which you may not have excelled. Be determined to be better and do the right thing. Over 200 years ago, Ben Franklin worked his precepts of order each evening. He wanted to be excellent and build his character even at a mature age.

38. Research ideas. What are your passions, and how do your ideas serve? Listen to your intuition and cultivate strategy. Look at what it would take to implement or be successful with your new ideas, then act on them,

implement the plan, review the plan and then improve it.

39. List streams of income and potential ways to serve and be prosperous. List how you will expand your life. Go past your comfort zones. List goals beyond your expectations and have deadlines of specificity. You can always change the date.

40. Review your lists and projects. Check off your accomplishments.

41. Meet with partners, family and/or spouse to define goals.

42. Discover your natural expression. What is your labor of love? Where do your passions lie? Remember that you work to pay bills, but you should always follow your dreams. Devote 20 percent of your waking hours each week to your passion. If you become great at it, odds are you can earn a living doing it too.

43. Choose and develop your character. How do you want to BE? Self-respect and self-regard can be developed and nurtured. When you rebuild yourself, you will in turn love yourself better, which allows you to be kinder, more generous and more loving to others.

44. With character comes responsibility toward your mental, physical and spiritual health. Do what works to take care of yourself with diet, exercise, learning, sleep, study and fellowship.

45. Associate with those who can help you where you can also help them. Create a network of business and spiritual friends.

46. Be good to yourself. Learn health self-regard and cultivate a loving relationship with the Source.

47. Teaching others not only helps them, but it helps you. Give away your knowledge in order to keep it.

48. Remember the Law of Increase. Radiate abundance, cheer and enthusiasm. Be contagious with love, cheer, and enthusiasm.

Chapter 8

It Works If You Work It

In this small chapter, we will divulge some of the greatest secrets to wealth and success ever known. Many people wonder why two people can be given the same recipe for happiness, and one gets rich and the other fails. By reading this booklet, you will be provided the power to follow your destiny. You will also be given the steps to success and the missing secrets to happiness that are utilized by the chosen few.

Results Will Prove You Right – Analyze, Diagnose and Clarify

Here we are focused on results and results ONLY. If the system works, then there is no refuting its POWER.

Half measures will avail you nothing. You must not be a wishful person, but rather a focused person filled with belief. Rather than sitting around thinking about what you would do if you won the lottery, maybe there is another way. Maybe the people that are relatively wealthy and happy are doing something different to achieve these coveted results?

Would you like a change? Do you want improvement? Are you willing to train your mind to new successful habits and character?

If you are ready, then there is a science to success and a clear and concise path to wealth, health and prosperity. All of us are using only a FRACTION of our abilities. Each one of us is a powerhouse of energy, consciousness, ideas and action.

From Pythagoras to Plato, from Spinoza to Hegel, and from Schopenhauer to Einstein, the great thinkers of all time imply the same thing. They claim that there are unseen cosmic forces that we can tap into that can energize and guide us to ideas, inventions, power and greatness.

Many of us want things but have we really been sincere? To achieve, we must be truly earnest about our goals. We must have that burning desire, which is something that you will go after and NEVER look back. This is a feeling of authentic PURPOSE where you will dedicate your whole heart to your betterment and becoming your best.

To make this big advancement, you must be willing to let go of your preconceptions. Give up your old ways and become open to a new path, new power and new abundance. What would you do if you could not fail? Truly ask yourself and petition your subconscious for inspiration and guidance. Ask for ideas, ask for help and ask for some sign that will lead you to new heights.

If you are willing to make this quantum leap, get out of your comfort zone and then learn a guaranteed method to riches and success if you are willing to put it to use with PERSISTENCE.

Unlimited Power is Yours

You have within you the power to connect to the universal force. This force is the creative and animating energy that permeates the universe. Like gravity or electricity, the force is not seen, but exists as the all-pervading framework upon which every law hinges. This interstellar force is also known as God or "The Life Force." This unlimited power is everywhere as creation is constant. New ideas, new art and music, new planets, new galaxies, new species, new worlds are continuously manifesting at this very moment.

That part of your mind that can be in tune with this force is referred to by the great teachers of metaphysics as the subjective mind or higher consciousness. Directed thought energy can be focused where the individual may act as a creative force within the universal framework. This supernatural power is willing to serve you and grant you anything that you earnestly and sincerely desire with focus, action, heartfelt gratitude and emotion. If faith is the substance of things hoped for, then that very substance can also be qualified as the energy of our attention and thoughts. Belief and faith are the same in that they mean that we accept what is unseen. Energy is consciousness, and thus, "thought awareness" is energy. All things created equally in perfect balance, the energy of faith, attention, and mind can tilt the cosmic balance of life, happiness and success in our favor.

This is why spiritual-metaphysics is so important because the participant who engages mental-cooperation with universal law attains the ability to optimize body, mind and spirit. The galactic framework of forces that we seek to cooperate with is what many call "the Spirit of the Universe" and "the Spirit within you." All of us go through life with a steady stream of ideas, thoughts and desires. Tapping into that greater, infinite self expands our intuitive abilities to best use our priceless inspiration. Thus, becoming aware that we may operate at a higher order of being is where achievement truly begins, and then we become willing to take the actions that provide results. Cooperation with the "force of the universe" and the framework of the metaphysical laws that affect mankind is the path to maximize our existence, contributions and consciousness. Learning to use the mind and concentrate on our desires is where self-actualization begins.

Even the great Marconi was referred to the insane asylum by government officials for suggesting that information and thoughts can be sent over the airwaves. However, today, all of us know that we can tune into any given channel and send messages millions of miles. Harnessing the power of prayer, meditation and contemplation is where inspiration and well-being is cultivated. With this power of mental focus and cooperation with the universal law, we become masters of our destiny.

The Master Key List – The Plan

Begin your new life today. Write out 5, 10 or even 50 things that you want to do to improve your life and circumstances. Don't be shy! Write the amazing and exciting things you will achieve about money, travel, relationships, health or whatever. Do it and do it today. As the great poet von Goethe once implied, begin it TODAY and there is MAGIC and POWER in it.

Write out your Master Key List and put it in your pocket. Think about it for a day, then pick the three most important things you can do to change your life for the better and begin immediately to commit to those three goals.

Every day, when you are in your Alpha Relaxed State, you can read the list to yourself. Read it at night and again upon awakening. Think about the completed successes, think about the ESSENCE of your purpose and how you can help yourself, your family and others by attaining your dreams.

As part of your continual growth, you can enhance, add, expand and remove things from your Master Key List.

A Mental Agreement for Specific Success

Your plans and mental blueprint should be very specific. For example, you can write out on a piece of paper a personal commitment to yourself:

I, [your name], will have a million-dollar business 5 years from today. I will sell super creative solutions. I will provide the best service and value to my customers. My products and services will have outstanding benefits for everyone. I will do my best, work hard and remain persistent. I will not falter. Everybody will be happy to pay me handsomely for my services because they will feel great benefits from what I/we provide. I will gladly accept compensation, and I will do what is needed to capture and utilize the funds. Sincerely, [YOUR NAME HERE]

Exercise: If we invoke the INNER POWER/SELF and EARNESTLY ask for help, harmony and cooperation, we are drawing closer to the Source. If we can meet the Source halfway, stay tuned into the POWER and cooperate with the Life Force, then our advancement will be speedy.

Exercise: Take some deep breaths... Your mental vibration is important. Can you take time to energize the way you feel about your goal? Think about a result that you want. Feel the joy of seeing it, sense it, and emotionalize it. See your desired result in your mind's eye. Visualize it. Think as if it is YOURS. Think grateful thoughts for the imagined result or something better being manifested in your life. Send the wonderful loving thoughts into the world with heartfelt gratitude, and knowing that the universe will bless you on your journey.

Definiteness of Purpose – Knowing what you want and dedicating yourself to it

Be definite about your desires. On your list:

1. Specify what the desire is. Examples: to weigh the same amount as you did when you graduated from high school, run a marathon, get a promotion or obtain a better home.
2. Identify exactly what you will do to achieve it.
3. Specify precisely when you will achieve it.
4. Determine what it will feel like to have it and what it will look like.
5. Imagine how you will use your success and envision what emotions you will have when you attain or use your desired outcome.
6. Take some concrete action to move toward your success each and every day.
7. If the desire is money, then specify the amount, what you will give in exchange for the money and how you will use or invest the money.

While you are building yourself up, associate with those who know about success. Ask encouraging people who know about what you want for help. Many will be happy to give you advice. Model yourself after the best and focus on the best as your belief system will certainly change for the better. Continue to use praise and appreciation in your life as this act of blessing all people and things expands your goodness, and brings prosperity and appreciation to you.

When you accomplish any little thing toward your happiness, recognize the goodness of the universe. Be grateful for every small achievement and bless each and every good event that comes your way. Gratitude dispels doubt, keeps you connected and prevents dissatisfaction. Continue to fix your attention on health, love, success and good fortune. Your faith will be renewed.

Sincere and heartfelt thankfulness will create a newfound faith in your abilities and will allow you to be connected to the great POWER within you.

Initiate Action – Using the Secret Methodology: Tips to Ensure Success

1. When you want something badly, be sure to allow the universe to bestow upon you the thing you want or something better. Do NOT limit the universe with your desires as the supernatural power may want to give you even more than you seek in new and untold ways.

2. Pray and meditate only for good to happen to yourself and others, and avoid negative thoughts or feelings for others or over any situation.

3. See the benefits and purpose of your desire and understand how your desire can help you and all involved, even going further to assist greater humanity.

4. Seize control of your Charisma and learn to direct and

master your personal magnetism.

5. Focus on being creative and not just competitive. You can win with your goals and desires by creating new opportunities for yourself and all people.

6. Try to maintain harmlessness in your actions, speech and thinking.

7. Maintain personal responsibility for your actions and take care of your spiritual condition.

8. Give without the expectation of receiving, and donate your time and talent to organizations that divinely inspire you and lift up your consciousness.

9. Give your attention to pressing needs first and then when you are stronger as a person, you can go for bigger and bigger goals.

10. Learn all you can to make yourself ready and capable to achieve any of your stated desires. However, remember to take action toward your goals NOW. Taking action can be as simple as reading a book, taking a course, calling somebody for an appointment or applying for a position.

11. Keep your consciousness and mental attitude clear and efficient. If you have done harm to others, try to make it right, and continuously maintain your well-being by maximizing the excellence of your character by practicing attunement and atonement.

12. Make a decision. Without commitment and making something important, the ideal will only be a hopeful wish. Your job is to go to the next level and make your move to achieve what you want with all your heart and desire.

13. Affirm your destiny. Speak it aloud to yourself every day. Say your positive affirmations and prayers out loud in the present tense with feeling and emotion. Speak constructively and learn to speak in an optimistic and confident way.

Remember, one of the greatest abilities of mankind is to give love. We live for the advancement of body, mind and soul, and there is no reason to limit our capacities. While many people see wealth as something for the greedy, poverty can and will frustrate your relationships with the spirit, other people and those you love. Accordingly, giving is one of the highest forms of love. Give yourself everything you need to become an asset to your community and to the world where one day you may give back as much as you can in great measure.

The Steps to Success – Moving Toward Your Destiny

1. Remember that growth, prosperity and the ability to innovate, create and adapt is your birthright. You are born to be prosperous and excellent.
2. Desire is a power seeking expression. You cannot desire what is not potentially within you; therefore, you can always be what you want to be.
3. Desire is the result of feeling, and the feeling that results from a burning desire is a supernatural faculty seeking and demanding greater expression.
4. Use your free time to hone your skills, improve your knowledge and prepare for your dreams and goals. Do not wait for the perfect opportunity to be all that you want to be. Become all that you can be today, and when an opportunity to be more is offered to you, be ready to take it.
5. Use your place or present business and environment as the means to get a better one. Spend nights and weekends cultivating your abilities and preparing for greater things and the fulfillment of your goals.
6. Everything that touches your life is an opportunity if you discover its proper use. Be aware of each circumstance and study them all, for they are your opportunities. Most men fail by hoping for some particular kind of luck

instead of being ready to seize opportunities.

7. Steadily hold the picture of all that you want to attain in person, property and environment. Form a clear conception of it. Then, understand that in so far as your desires are not contrary to Eternal Justice, it is absolutely certain that you can be what you want to be. Dwell upon your goal and ideal until it is clear and definite to you, and hold it until it arouses intense desire.

8. Your vision of the right idea, if held with faith and purpose, will cause the Supreme Intelligence to move the right opportunity toward you. Then your action, if performed with effectiveness and efficiency, will cause you to move toward success.

9. Pray with unfaltering grateful faith to the Supreme Intelligence that your desires shall come to you, practicing thankfulness in every prayer, petition or affirmation. Express thanksgiving with a heart full of gratitude that your desires are coming to you.

10. Think about this ideal picture until you are perpetually conscious of it with positive emotion. Mentally presume it is yours.

11. Desire for everybody what you want for yourself. Be sure to take nothing from anybody without giving back a full equivalent in life and value; the more you give, the better for you.

12. Use each day to the fullest and do each act efficiently and effectively without haste, putting expanding thoughts into everything you do, communicating excellence to all with whom you deal.

13. Know that others from around the world desire to help you now that you are on the supernatural path. You are to cooperate and be willing to receive this mutually beneficial exchange and assistance from those who are sent to you.

14. The basic element of success is, therefore, to hold the thought and the mental attitude of advancement and to be excellent in all that you do.

15. Strive to maintain a consciousness of your being at one with the Spiritual Power of the Universe. Know that you are connected to the Creative Power and begin now to co-create your destiny with it.

So the questions are these: How do you become great? How do you become wealthy? How do you become successful?

After years of research, we find that most great teachers will give you the quantum mechanics of success. They say things like, "If you do certain things, you'll get certain outcomes. If you model yourself after the best, you'll get the highest rewards. If you perform the technicalities or the practical motions to attain certain consequences, you will become what you want to become. Therefore, if you go to the gym and do various and specific exercises every day results will unfold. Then, at the end of several months you'll have an optimal body, according to what you have desired or what you have planned." The real issue of the day, though, is that many people are discouraged because they don't see the results of their work in the short-term or, once they feel a little better, they quit the new regimen. But remember, just like going to the gym, whether it's a mental gymnasium or the physical gymnasium, if you go to the gym and you're working out every day, at the end of 30 days, you have probably made great advances, but your body is still in transformation. Other people may notice that you've made great changes, but you may not notice yet. That's often how these transformations occur – one day at a time, one action at a time, one task at a time. With focus, we can improve just about any facet of our lives. By taking these steps, each of us will make the best of ourselves on the level of body, mind and spirit.

This guide can create that shift and awakening that you have wanted to achieve for years. Act now and obtain the secrets for success. Keep this book close, study it and become a master of your destiny.

Chapter 9

Conclusion: 12 Steps to Fulfillment – Qualities of enlightened individuals who are living their dreams

1. **Spiritual Mind** – People who live in abundance mentally are those who put their spiritual consciousness before their ego. People who are able to do this tend to live more authentically and more effectively because the mind is not clouding or limiting their cognitive abilities. These people are successful because they understand that growth is an inside job, and if they can improve themselves, then all will benefit.

2. **Knowingness** – Knowing that the world is an abundant place is also an empowering vibration. A common thread with those who believe in unlimited opportunities are those who focus on the truth of abundance, the truth of opportunity and the facts related to an abundant world. This belief energizes people to never quit, who persist and seek more from life. People who engage knowingness effectively use constructive aspiration. They know that they have choices and power over their decisions and the way that they think.

3. **Contemplative Action** – We should detach from any concepts of limitation or unworthiness, and get into action. People engaged in constructive activities are taking steps each day toward their goals. They tend to be the people who follow their dreams and complete big ideas. Life's successes are generally one step at a time, one day at a time. As such, people who finish big things are

usually beginning with boldness and crossing the finish line consistently with each small step.

4. **Righteous Speech** – Use words constructively during your daily life, and attempt at all times to speak and think in ways that are related to progress, opportunity and potential. Our words should be focused around absolute possibility.

5. **Be Excellence & Do Excellence** – We must do each act in a superior way and in an excellent way. We have to BECOME the best person we each can be and BECOME what we desire. Be GREAT TO YOURSELF. This concept is focused on self-regard, but we also want to cultivate personal regard for everything around us and develop a harmonious relationship with ourselves, our neighbors and with the universe.

6. **Co-Creation and Ideas** – All of us want to find true purpose and have a livelihood that is meaningful. If we are in cooperation with the world and the universe, this harmony will allow inspiration that leads to ideas and creativity that affect the universe in a creative and productive manner.

7. **Flow** – Circulate your good and empower others. This power begins with helping others find the best in themselves and circulating your good. Giving of ourselves, such as giving away our services, teaching, donating excess items or giving to organizations and people who divinely inspire us does exactly that, and results in success for everyone. If we hoard our good and our knowledge, the generous transfer of insights and business from others can be stifled.

8. **Detachment and Acceptance** – For many of us, we must learn to accept the way many things are, but we also need to accept the opportunities and blessings. Many of us have great hopes or ideas for our lives; however, some people are not comfortable accepting success and greatness. If we can develop a worthiness of our ideal outcomes in mind, the possibilities are increased. We alone are responsible for cultivating a detached acceptance and consciousness of what we want to be and have. By doing so, the mental equivalent is produced to allow for the manifestation of our desires. Clarity is needed and detachment from the world's follies will allow us to have the awareness and mindset to receive the good that desires to come to us.

9. **Mind Your Business** – Invest in yourself and other people. Every one of us comes to the point where we are deciding how to allocate our resources, how to allocate our time, our energy and our money; and many of us who have become successful are those who have figured out ways to focus on investing in ourselves, becoming better people, learning new skills, learning what is going on in society and humanity, and learning how to maximize our contribution to the world and operating in a way that is a labor of love. Those who are doing these things are the ones who are living out their true purpose and living authentically, as they have the type of positive occupational therapy that benefits themselves and other people. As a byproduct of that activity, they are rewarded handsomely.

10. **Give Increase to All** – What does increase mean? It means in all that you do, whether it is in your personal life or your business life, you give more than is expected of you.

Give quality service and value to all people with whom you interact. In this way, people will respect everything that you do because you are providing excellence and you are providing augmentation in the lives of others. Let's just say, for example, that you're continually providing people with better methods or better products or services that make their lives easier. You are providing solutions, and when you provide solutions, you are benefiting humanity.

11. **Character Expansion** – Thinking, action and omission. How do these concepts interrelate? In essence, your character is YOU. Thus, you are what you think, you are what do and you are what you do not do. The totality of your actions and inactions becomes your character. This means that if you focus on cultivating a character that is at a higher level, you will create a worldview that is at a higher level. Therefore, the greater your spiritual condition, the greater your worldview and your journey and experience. Your character defines your view or your perception, and your perception defines your experience – it is all tied together. Taking better care of your thoughts and actions directly translates into more opportunities for prosperity and excellence.

12. **Bless Your World** – Bless other people, bless yourself, seek a state of love and gratitude. Gratitude is not only being thankful for what you have and having a thankful mind and thankful heart, but it is also cultivating a grateful mind and a grateful attitude where we are being appreciative of ourselves, our attributes and who we are. It also is appreciating other people and being thankful for other individuals, places and things. This secret involves having that harmonious, appreciative and grateful

attitude toward our surroundings. Claim your divine abundance by having a mindset of fulfillment and growth. Knowing that you have enough in your life and that you're complete and whole is one of the keys to living in harmony and living in gratitude. Each day is another opportunity for change, growth, innovation and unique expression. Overall, be on the lookout for the signs and miracles of the universe.

Lastly, learn to be a powerful ray of sunshine to those around you. Radiate peace and empowerment. As they say, the more you bless other people around you in mind and deed, the odds are in your favor that they will want the best for you as well.

Chapter 10

Quotes on Prosperity and Abundance

These wise quotes from the masters, both old and new, will help you on your path to prosperity and success in everything you do. Learn them, identify with them and keep them close as you travel on your journey.

"It is wealth to be content."
– Lao Tzu

"Wealth is not his that has it, but his who enjoys it."
– Benjamin Franklin

"Life is a field of unlimited possibilities."
– Deepak Chopra

"He who is plenteously provided for from within, needs but little from without."
– Johann Wolfgang von Goethe

"Take full account of the excellencies which you possess, and in gratitude remember how you would hanker after them, if you had them not."
– Marcus Aurelius

"Whenever anything negative happens to you, there is a deep lesson concealed within it, although you may not see it at the time."
– Eckhart Tolle

"If you want to change who you are, begin by changing the size of your dream. Even if you are broke, it does not cost you anything to dream of being rich. Many poor people are poor because they have given up on dreaming."
– Robert Kiyosaki

"Ideas are the beginning points of all fortunes."
– Napoleon Hill

"When you are grateful, fear disappears and abundance appears."
– Anthony Robbins

"Everything in the universe has a purpose. Indeed, the invisible intelligence that flows through everything in a purposeful fashion is also flowing through you."
– Dr. Wayne Dyer

"Gratitude is an attitude that hooks us up to our source of supply. And the more grateful you are, the closer you become to your maker, to the architect of the universe, to the spiritual core of your being. It's a phenomenal lesson."
– Bob Proctor

"Living in Abundance and Prosperity is a Reasonable Option."
– Magus Incognito

"You have a divine right to abundance, and if you are anything less than a millionaire, you haven't had your fair share."
– Stuart Wilde

"Prosperity is not just having things. It is the consciousness that attracts the things. Prosperity is a way of living and thinking, and not just having money or things. Poverty is a way of living and thinking, and not just a lack of money or things."
– Eric Butterworth

"Most folks are about as happy as they make up their minds to be."
– Abraham Lincoln

"And he shall be like a tree planted by the rivers of water, that bringeth forth his fruit in his season; his leaf also shall not wither; and whatsoever he doeth shall prosper."
– Psalm 1:3

"The Constitution only gives people the right to pursue happiness. You have to catch it yourself."
– Benjamin Franklin

"Not what we have But what we enjoy, constitutes our abundance."
– Epicurus

"Gratitude is the vital ingredient in the recipe for Faith."
– Magus Incognito

"We may divide thinkers into those who think for themselves and those who think through others. The latter are the rule and the former the exception. The first are original thinkers in a double sense, and egotists in the noblest meaning of the word."
– Arthur Schopenhauer

"The key to every man is his thought. Sturdy and defiant though he look he has a helm which he obeys, which is the idea after which all his facts are classified. He can only be reformed by showing him a new idea which commands his own."
– Ralph Waldo Emerson

"All truly wise thoughts have been thought already thousands of times; but to make them really ours we must think them over again honestly till they take root in our personal expression."
– Johann Wolfgang von Goethe

"Great men are they who see that spirituality is stronger than any material force; that thoughts rule the world."
– Ralph Waldo Emerson

"All that we are is a result of what we have thought."
– Buddha

"Wealth is the slave of a wise man. The master of a fool."
– Seneca

"Happiness is not in the mere possession of money; it lies in the joy of achievement, in the thrill of creative effort."
– Franklin D. Roosevelt

"Money is like manure. You have to spread it around or it smells."
– J. Paul Getty

"Liberty is not a means to a higher political end. It is the highest political end."
– Lord John Dalberg-Acton

"We are what we repeatedly do. Excellence, then, is not an act but a habit."
– Aristotle

"Money is like love; it kills slowly and painfully the one who withholds it, and enlivens the other who turns it on his fellow man."
– Kahlil Gibran

"Empty pockets never held anyone back. Only empty heads and empty hearts can do that."
– Norman Vincent Peale

"The thief cometh not, but for to steal, and to kill, and to destroy: I am come that they might have life, and that they might have it more abundantly."
– John 10:10, KJV

"Prosperity is not without many fears and distastes, and adversity is not without comforts and hopes."
– Francis Bacon

"It is health that is real wealth and not pieces of gold and silver."
– Mahatma Gandhi

"Desire is the starting point of all achievement, not a hope, not a wish, but a keen pulsating desire, which transcends everything. When your desires are strong enough you will appear to possess superhuman powers to achieve."
– Napoleon Hill

"Move out of your comfort zone. You can only grow if you are willing to feel awkward and uncomfortable when you try something new."
– Brian Tracy

"You can open your mind to prosperity when you realize the true definition of the word: You are prosperous to the degree you are experiencing peace, health and plenty in your world."
– Catherine Ponder, *Open Your Mind to Prosperity*

"There is a science of getting rich and it is an exact science, like algebra or arithmetic. There are certain laws which govern the process of acquiring riches and once these laws are learned and obeyed by anyone, that person will get rich with mathematical certainty."
– Wallace D. Wattles

"Within you right now is the power to do things you never dreamed possible. This power becomes available to you just as soon as you can change your beliefs."
– Dr. Maxwell Maltz

"Far better it is to dare mighty things, to win glorious triumphs even though checkered by failure, than to rank with those timid spirits who neither enjoy nor suffer much because they live in the gray twilight that knows neither victory nor defeat."
– President Theodore Roosevelt

Chapter 11

Two Final Exercises

1) A Final Visualization Exercise for Results

1. In a quiet spot, enter your relaxed state of mind and take a few deep breaths.
2. Relax each part of the body, one by one.
3. Close your eyes and imagine a snapshot of something that you really want to happen in your life.
4. Detail the final result of this desire with your five senses. View it, smell it, hear it, taste it, and touch it in your MIND.
5. Imagine the emotions that you will have when this dream or goal or result is reached. Feel the emotions of joy and thankfulness.
6. Harvest the mental essence of how having the result or thing will function in your life, how it will serve you and how it will help all involved.
7. Believe that it has happened in your mind and allow yourself to imagine the present ownership of this result.
8. Pinpoint and focus on the completed final event of success. For example, "The foot race is completed," or "The check is in your bank account." You are also encouraged to imagine the incremental successes and steps being achieved along with the arrival at the final result.
9. Experience love and grateful feelings when you recognize and realize your vision. Know and feel it as if it is fact.
10. Imagine the benefits for all involved.
11. Be willing to receive all of this good on a mental and spiritual level, which allows you to take actions toward creating and receiving the results.

12. Make sure you have created ways to capture the result. Example: You may not be able to become the highest paid pilot without a license. Also, allow yourself to feel deserving and worthy of the result.

13. Send this mental vision into the world with joy as a mental letter delivered to the Supreme Architect.

14. Respond to communication from others and ponder your intuition. Be willing to meet others halfway and to go the extra mile.

15. Allow your dreams to unfold on parallel lines. Example: You may want a successful business in offering one product or service, but the laws of attraction and excellence may allow you to sell many other things related to it.

2) Character Building Exercises to Ask Yourself

1. Are your spirit, mind and body in an ideal condition? If not, what do you want to do this year to expand your present situation?

2. Have you studied the things you wanted to learn about? Will you continue?

3. Have you seen the things you are most interested in? The art, the places, the people?

4. What type of career or careers are you most suited for? If you could pick two or three careers that you would love to do, what would they be?

5. If you could not fail, what would you do with your life?

6. Do you have anxiety or fears about your career or relationships? If so, why? What can you do to lower the stress and improve your enjoyment of life?

7. How do you want to be treated by others? What can you do to improve the way you are perceived?

8. Can you think of three people you have loved as a good friend?

9. In the Beatles song, *The End*, the lyrics state, "And in the end, the love you take is equal to the love you make." Are you giving or radiating love? Are you giving a reasonable amount of love and praise to those you love?

10. What is the one thing that you could improve about yourself that would make the greatest difference in your opportunity or appearance?

11. At the end of your life, how would you want people to remember you?

12. Where do you want to travel? What do you want to see before you get too old? What do you want your children to see?

13. Remember five things that you are grateful for in your childhood – people, family, experiences, talents. Remember that feeling of awe, excitement and appreciation that you once had.

14. If you could model yourself after one or two successful people, who would they be and why?

15. Who are you? How would you define yourself?

16. Do you feel worthy of an excellent life? What could you do to improve your outlook on life?

17. What five things can you do each day that would allow you to treat other people better and to feel better about yourself?

18. What can you feed yourself to make you healthier, happier and smarter? Include things like food, news, literature, exercise and types of relationships.

19. Name 10 hobbies or activities that you enjoy. Examples: puzzles, tennis, bowling, reciting poetry. Do some of them. Get out of your comfort zone and explore.

20. What spiritually inspires you? What makes you feel more in tune with the universe? What gives you peace and harmony? How could you donate your talent, time or money to something that inspires you?

Appendix A

Concise Chronology of Esoteric Spirituality

Here is a basic timetable of Esoteric Spirituality and Gnosticism:

1. Heraclitus: 6th Century BC
2. Pythagoras: Born 571 BC, Greece – Italy
3. Laozi: Lao Tzu – Taoism; Born 571 BC
4. Confucius: Born 551 BC
5. Siddhartha Gautama: Buddhism; 6th Century BC, India
6. Socrates, Plato, Aristotle: 5th–4th Centuries BC
7. Epicurus: 4th Century BC
8. Cicero: 43 BC
9. Marcus Aurelius: 180 AD
10. Iamblichus: 300 AD
11. St. Benedict: 5th Century
12. Scottus (Johannes Scotus Erigena): 9th Century
13. Hildegard von Bingen: 11th Century
14. Meister Eckhart: 13th Century Mystic
15. Jan Hus, Jacob Boehme: Moravian Piety, 13th–17th Centuries
16. Rosicrucians: 14th Century
17. Martin Luther: 16th Century
18. Baruch Spinoza: 1632–1677
19. Nikolaus Ludwig von Zinzendorf und Pottendorf: 18th Century
20. Leibniz: 1710
21. Hegel: 1807
22. Schopenhauer: 1818
23. Emerson and Thoreau: 1860s – American Transcendentalism
24. Judge Thomas Troward: 1900
25. Carl Jung: Gnostic Mysticism

26. Dr. Samuel M. Shoemaker: Oxford Movement 1900–1940s
27. 12-Step Programs: 1930s
28. Wayne Dyer, Eckhart Tolle: 21st Century, "The Secret" Speakers

Many more people could be included in this chronology as this is a short and generalized list.

Appendix B

Quotes by Famous Physicists and Scientists on Spirituality

"I am very astonished that the scientific picture of the real world around me is very deficient. It gives a lot of factual information, puts all our experiences in a magnificently consistent order, but is ghastly silent about all and sundry that is really near to our heart, that really matters to us. It cannot tell us a word about red and blue, bitter and sweet, physical pain and physical delight; it knows nothing of beautiful and ugly, good or bad, God and eternity."
– Erwin Schroedinger (1887–1961)

"I find it as difficult to understand a scientist who does not acknowledge the presence of a superior rationality behind the existence of the universe as it is to comprehend a theologian who would deny the advances of science."
– Wernher von Braun (1912–1977), German-American rocket scientist

"Science can have a purifying effect on religion, freeing it from beliefs of a pre-scientific age and helping us to a truer conception of God. At the same time, I am far from believing that science will ever give us the answers to all our questions."
– Nevill Mott (1905–1996), English physicist, awarded Nobel Prize in 1977

"The gift of mental power comes from God, Divine Being, and if we concentrate our minds on that truth, we become in tune with this great power."
– Nikola Tesla; Tesla was the winner of: Edison Medal (1916); Elliott Cresson Medal (1894); John Scott Medal (1934)

"Something which is against natural laws seems to me rather out of the question because it would be a depressive idea about God. It would make God smaller than he must be assumed. When he stated that these laws hold, then they hold, and he wouldn't make exceptions. This is too human an idea. Humans do such things, but not God."

– Max Born, who was instrumental in the development of quantum mechanics; Nobel Prize winning physicist

"The first gulp from the glass of natural sciences will turn you into an atheist, but at the bottom of the glass God is waiting for you."

– Werner Heisenberg, 1932 Nobel Prize in Physics for the creation of quantum mechanics

"… Those laws are within the grasp of the human mind. God wanted us to recognize them by creating us after his own image so that we could share in his own thoughts… and if piety allow us to say so, our understanding is in this respect of the same kind as the divine, at least as far as we are able to grasp something of it in our mortal life."

– Johannes Kepler, the German mathematician and astronomer who is considered to be one of the founders of the field of astronomy

"Whence it follows that God is absolutely perfect, since perfection is nothing but magnitude of positive reality, in the strict sense, setting aside the limits or bounds in things which are limited."

– Gottfried Leibniz, the German mathematician and philosopher (1646–1716) who founded calculus

"The best data we have (concerning the Big Bang) are exactly what I would have predicted, had I nothing to go on but the five books of Moses, the Psalms, the Bible as a whole."

– Arno Penzias, the 1978 Nobel Prize recipient in physics

"Another source of conviction in the existence of God, connected with the reason and not with the feelings, impresses me as having much more weight. This follows from the extreme difficulty or rather impossibility of conceiving this immense and wonderful universe, including man with his capacity of looking far backwards and far into futurity, as the result of blind chance or necessity. When thus reflecting I feel compelled to look to a First Cause having an intelligent mind in some degree analogous to that of man; and I deserve to be called a Theist."
– Charles Darwin, the founder of evolutionary biology, as quoted in his autobiography

"To know the mighty works of God, to comprehend His wisdom and majesty and power; to appreciate, in degree, the wonderful workings of His laws, surely all this must be a pleasing and acceptable mode of worship to the Most High, to whom ignorance cannot be more grateful than knowledge."
– Nicolaus Copernicus, the mathematician and astronomer (1473–1543)

"Science is a game – but a game with reality, a game with sharpened knives. If a man cuts a picture carefully into 1000 pieces, you solve the puzzle when you reassemble the pieces into a picture; in the success or failure, both your intelligences compete. In the presentation of a scientific problem, the other player is the good Lord. He has not only set the problem but also has devised the rules of the game – but they are not completely known, half of them are left for you to discover or to deduce. The uncertainty is how many of the rules God himself has permanently ordained, and how many apparently are caused by your own mental inertia, while the solution generally becomes possible only through freedom from its limitations. This is perhaps the most exciting thing in the game."
– Erwin Schroedinger, winner of the 1933 Nobel Prize in Physics

"The atoms or elementary particles themselves are not real; they form a world of potentialities or possibilities rather than one of things or facts."
– Werner Heisenberg

"Science is not only compatible with spirituality; it is a profound source of spirituality. When we recognize our place in an immensity of light-years and in the passage of ages, when we grasp the intricacy, beauty, and subtlety of life, then that soaring feeling, that sense of elation and humility combined, is surely spiritual... The notion that science and spirituality are somehow mutually exclusive does a disservice to both."
– Carl Sagan (1934–1996)

"Observations not only disturb what is to be measured, they produce it."
– Pascual Jordan

All quotes attributed and assumed to be the sayings of the author.

About George Mentz

George Mentz is a premier, sought-after speaker, revolutionary author, and global management consultant. Dr. Mentz is universally referenced by his clientele, friends and colleagues as one of the most thoughtful, enthusiastic and empathetic leaders in the business world today. George Mentz, an international lawyer and passionate professor, is the founder of the GAFM Global Academy of Financial Management® and he has published extensively in the fields of law, e-business, SEO, entrepreneurship, marketing, international finance, and success strategy. George Mentz has advised and consulted with the US Government, United Nations and Fortune 500 companies on domestic and international strategy while helping people from around the world improve their education and careers.

George Mentz and his companies have held seminars and VIP courses in over 35 countries worldwide. Professor Mentz received his Doctor of Jurisprudence and MBA degrees after attending legal and business coursework at Loyola University, Université catholique Belgium, William and Mary Law School, Tulane University in the USA, Austria, Spain, Mexico and Brazil. Mentz is the first person in the United States to achieve "Quad Designation" Status as a JD, MBA, qualified/licensed financial planner and wealth manager, and Qualified/Certified Financial Consultant and Planner. Counselor Mentz is the recipient of national awards and honors for his contributions in the fields of management, excellence, teaching, charity, leadership and speaking. In recent years, George Mentz has been named an expert and leader for his publications and he has been honored by mainstream media as a brain trust member and part of the Dream Team of Financial Writers for mainstream media outlets. George Mentz has served on the advisory boards of: the Global Finance Forum in Switzerland, the World E-Commerce Forum in the UK, the Certified Economist Association of Africa, and the China Wealth Management Institute of Hong Kong, the Arab Academy Standards Council, the International Project Management Commission, a US medical school, a law school's Graduate Program, and various charities. Mentz is a syndicated author and two-time national award-winning professor, and is a contributor and expert for various organizations where some of Dr. Mentz's bestselling books and publications include: *CWM Chartered Wealth Manager Guide*, *Project Manager Executive Guide*, "Internet College Recruiting and Marketing", *The Wealth Management Executive Guide*, Online Credibility in the Finance World – Protecting Your Web Reputation & Company Brand, *The Secret Powers of Highly Effective People*, *Spiritual Wealth Management*, *Wealth Management and Financial Planning*, and many more. Published in many journals, Mentz is a pioneer in the movements of: executive certification training, international wealth management, internet marketing and human-potential through neuroplasticity. Mentz and his executive development companies are accredited by the TUV Austria, ISO Certified for Quality, and have been featured or quoted in the NASDAQ News, *Forbes*, *Reuters*, *Morningstar*, Yahoo Finance, *Wall Street Globe*, the *Hindu National*, *El Norte* Latin America, the *Financial Times*, *NYSSA New York Securities Analysts News*, the *ChinaDaily*, the Department of Education ERIC Library, the US Department of Labor Brochures, *Black Enterprise*, the *San Francisco Chronicle*, *Associated Press* and the *Arab Times*.

http://www.GeorgeMentz.com

You can contact Dr.jur. GS Mentz at his website,
www.gmentz.com
on Linkedin.com at
https://www.linkedin.com/in/georgementz
or at O-Books.com

For Speaking Engagements, Prof./Counselor Mentz discusses several key topics such as: Wealth Management, Quantum Bliss and Success, Innovation and Leadership using Quantum Principles.

Other References or Authors of Interest

1.   Allen, J. (1998) *As You Think*. Ed. with introduction by M. Allen. Novato, CA: New World Library
2.   Behrend, G. (1927) *Your Invisible Power*. Montana: Kessinger Publishing
3.   Carlson, R. (2001) *Don't Sweat the Small Stuff About Money*. New York: Hyperion. Previously published as *Don't Worry, Make Money*.
     http://www.dontsweat.com
4.   Carnegie, D. (1994) *How to Win Friends and Influence People*. New York: Pocket Books.
     http://www.dalecarnegie.com
5.   Chopra, D. (1996) *The Seven Spiritual Laws of Success*. London: Bantam Press.
     http://www.chopra.com
6.   Collier, R. (1970) *Be Rich!* Oak Harbor, WA: Robert Collier Publications.
     http://robertcollierpublications.com
7.   Covey, SR (1989) *The 7 Habits of Highly Effective People*. London: Simon & Schuster.
     http://www.stephencovey.com
8.   Dyer, W. (1993) *Real Magic: Creating Miracles in Everyday Life*. New York: HarperCollins.
     http://www.drwaynedyer.com
9.   Gawain, Shakti (1979) *Creative Visualization*. Mill Valley: Whatever Publishing.
     http://www.shaktigawain.com
10. Hill, Napoleon (1960) *Think and Grow Rich*. New York: Fawcett Crest
11. Hill, Napoleon, WD Wattles, R. Collier et al (2010) *How to Be Rich*. US: Tarcher/Penguin.
     http://www.tarcherbooks.net/new-release-how-to-be-rich

12. His Holiness the Dalai Lama & Howard C. Cutler (1999) *The Art of Happiness: A Handbook for Living*. London: Hodder & Stoughton.
http://www.dalailama.com

13. James, William (1902) *The Varieties of Religious Experience*. New York: Penguin

14. Maltz, Maxwell, MD (1960) *Psycho-Cybernetics*. New York: Pocket Books

15. Marden, OS (1997) *Pushing to the Front, or Success under Difficulties*, Vols 1 & 2. Santa Fe, CA: Sun Books

16. Mentz et al (2006) *How to Master Abundance and Prosperity – The* Master Key System *Decoded*. Bloomington, IN: Xlibris

17. Mentz et al (2007) *MASTERS OF THE SECRETS: The Science of Getting Rich & Master Key System Expanded Bestseller Version*. Bloomington, IN: Xlibris

18. Mentz, GS (2013) *Spiritual Wealth Management: The Abundance Bible & Prosperity Manifesto*. Bloomington, IN: Balboa Press

19. Mentz, George (2014) *The Edge: Managing Your Client's Financial Well-being in Risky Times*. New York: National Underwriter Publishing

20. Mulford, Prentice (1908) *Thoughts are Things – Essays Selected From The White Cross Library*. Manchester, CT: Seed-Of-Life-Publishing

21. Murphy, J. (1963) *The Power of Your Subconscious Mind*. New Jersey: Prentice Hall

22. Ponder, C. (1962) *The Dynamic Laws of Prosperity*. Camarillo, CA: DeVorss & Co

23. Price, JR (1987) *The Abundance Book*. Carlsbad, CA: Hay House.
http://www.johnrandolphprice.com

24. Roman, S. and Packer, D. (1988) *Creating Money*. Tiburon, CA: Kramer.

http://www.orindaben.com

25. Smiles, S. (2002) *Self-Help: With Illustrations of Conduct and Perseverance.* Oxford, UK: Oxford University Press

26. Tracy, B. (1993) *Maximum Achievement: Strategies and Skills That Will Unlock Your Hidden Powers to Succeed.* New York: Fireside.

http://www.briantracy.com

27. Troward, Judge Thomas (1904) *The Edinburgh Lectures on Mental Science*

28. Wattles, WD (1976) *Financial Success through the Power of Creative Thought* [*The Science of Getting Rich*]. Rochester, Vermont: Destiny Books. (Written originally around 1910)

Disclaimer

This work consists of original works created from analyzing the philosophy of the great teachers of the past, and the creative revision, original insights, revised or updated public domain works, or the enhancement of the philosophy of Pythagoras, Marcus Aurelius, Meister Eckhart, Von Goethe, Judge Thomas Troward, Genevieve Behrend, Christian Larson, Hegel, Schopenhauer, William Walker Atkinson, Magus Incognito, and many others from ancient history. From the Dark Ages to the Reformation and Enlightenment, the world began to study, interpret and deliver universal truth, tactics of prosperity and secrets of obtaining peace of mind. Some pre-1925 public domain concepts are contained herein along with timeless ideas which cannot be attributed.

All readers are advised to find a licensed professional before making any important medical, legal, health, tax or financial decision. Always seek the advice of a competent counsel or physician with any questions you may have regarding a medical issue. Advice must be tailored to the specific circumstances of each person and case, and laws and advice are constantly changing. No legal, health or medical advice is intended to be given in this book. The advice in this book are generalized suggestions where many have benefited from implementing various ideas herein.

The Greatest Success Secrets Ever Known! VIP GUIDE
~ *Many are Called but Few are Chosen* ~

The wisdom in this document is based on conversations with some of the world's richest and most influential people. Over a 25-year period, we have met with Billionaires, Princes, Kings, CEOs, Sheikhs, Navy Seals, Ambassadors, Rock Stars, Judges, Cabinet Members, Pro MVPs, Bishops, TV Celebrities, Hollywood Producers, World Famous Musicians, Luminary Professors, Artists, Presidents, Potentates and some of the most successful authors in the world. The results of these conversations are contained in this small booklet. May this guide help you in your desire for fulfillment, abundance and peace beginning on this special day.

This book is a short summary of timeless success principles that have been proven to work for thousands of years. It is up to you to use them for the betterment of your life and conditions. In this small guide, we will divulge some of the greatest secrets to wealth and success ever known. Many people wonder why two people can be given the same recipe for happiness, and one gets rich and the other fails. By reading this booklet, you will be provided the power to follow your destiny. You will also be given the steps to success and the missing secrets to happiness that are utilized by the chosen few.

George Mentz, JD, MBA, CWM, DSS, International Lawyer
Written by a former top wealth advisor of a Wall Street firm

BOOKS

O is a symbol of the world, of oneness and unity; this eye represents knowledge and insight. We publish titles on general spirituality and living a spiritual life. We aim to inform and help you on your own journey in this life.

Visit our website: http://www.o-books.com

Find us on Facebook:
https://www.facebook.com/OBooks

Follow us on Twitter: @obooks